Beyond "I Do"

WHAT CHRISTIANS BELIEVE
ABOUT MARRIAGE

Douglas J. Brouwer

William B. Eerdmans Publishing Company
Grand Rapids, Michigan / Cambridge, U.K.

Wm. B. Eerdmans Publishing Co.
255 Jefferson Ave. S.E., Grand Rapids, Michigan 49503 /
P.O. Box 163, Cambridge CB3 9PU U.K.

Printed in the United States of America

06 05 04 03 02 01   7 6 5 4 3 2 1

www.eerdmans.com

Library of Congress Cataloging-in-Publication Data

Brouwer, Douglas J.
Beyond "I do" : what Christians believe about marriage /
Douglas J. Brouwer.
p.   cm.
ISBN 0-8028-4806-0 (pbk. : alk. paper)
1. Marriage — Religious aspects — Christianity. I. Title.
BT706 .B755 2001
248.4 — dc21
2001040310

Contents

CONTENTS

Acknowledgments

My thanks to the following people who in many ways, large and small, contributed to this book and helped to make it better than it would have been without their help.

I'm grateful, first of all, to the Louisville Institute for the generous grant I received. I am grateful in a particular way to Associate Director David Wood for his personal encouragement to use the grant in a way that I found refreshing and renewing for my ministry. I certainly tried. The Lilly Endowment, which made the grant money available, has a wonderful vision for encouraging pastors in their ministry.

I'm grateful also to the members and staff of First Presbyterian Church of Wheaton. They made it possible for me to disengage from my ministry and to use my accumulated study leave in one large chunk. Being away from the church for an entire summer of writing and reflecting renewed me in a way that has already given me new life and fresh vision for my ministry.

The writers group that I've been involved with for several years has been one of the unexpected pleasures of my life. The encouragement and challenge I receive from them keeps me going and pushes me to be a better writer than I would otherwise be. I'm grateful to Michele Hempel and Patricia Locke, who have read every word of this book with care and discernment.

Several people graciously agreed to read the book at an early stage. Their comments and suggestions were helpful, and occasionally they pushed me to insights I didn't know I had in me. I'm grateful beyond words to Jim Luzadder, Kathy Fuller, Don and Linda Sloat, Kate Lindberg, Mary Talen, and Tom Dozeman. I have terrific and loving friends.

Anita Eerdmans, Amanda Dombek, Jon Pott, and in particular my editor, Mary Hietbrink — all part of William B. Eerdmans Publishing Company — have been wonderful to work with, and I am grateful for the knowledge, skill, and good humor that they bring to their work.

Finally, I'm grateful to my wife. I enjoy being married, and I enjoy being married to Susan in particular. I have found our life together to be immeasurably rich — far better and far richer than my life alone would have been. Susan is my best friend, confidante, and lover. I am grateful for the gift that our marriage has been to me, and I hope I live gratefully because of what I have experienced. I couldn't have written a book about marriage with a sense of wonder and appreciation if it were not for our life together. I dedicate this book to her.

How I Came to Write This Book

One fall not long ago, I taught a ten-week adult education class on marriage at my church. I expected a strong interest and wasn't disappointed. After all, programs on topics like marriage and parenting are popular in a suburban church like mine. Often people want even more than we already offer.

What I wasn't prepared for was the depth of interest people showed and the seriousness with which they participated. Many couples came together and sat together in class. Many took notes. Whenever I referred to specific verses from the Bible, most followed along in their own Bibles, paying careful attention to each word I read.

Because the class was large, the only space at the church that could accommodate us was the sanctuary, which for many reasons is not an ideal setting for large-group discussion. As a result, several people e-mailed me during the week with additional questions, comments, and observations about the class.

At times I was overwhelmed by the sheer intensity of those who participated. In the beginning I started each class with prayer, and then I told a corny joke about marriage, hoping to balance the seriousness of the topic with something light. But after the first few weeks I stopped telling jokes. I came to realize something that I suppose I already knew but didn't fully appreciate. Marriage is an important issue in the lives of most people —

and certainly in the lives of the members of my church. It's no laughing matter. And church is certainly no comedy club. The people who came to my class had come to get answers to some difficult and vexing questions.

I assume the people in my church are probably not so different from those in other churches. Christian people think about marriage a great deal, especially their own marriages. They talk about marriage, they read about marriage, they pray about marriage, and many of them, I'm aware, *worry* about marriage — not just their own marriages but the marriages of people they care about. I now know from teaching my class that Christian people even worry about the meaning of marriage itself. They can see for themselves, as I have, that marriage has changed and is continuing to change. And so they wonder what these changes mean both for themselves and for others.

In my own lifetime I've noticed subtle — and at times not-so-subtle — changes in the way people think about marriage. People older than I am tend to regard marriage differently from people younger than I am. Changes in the social, cultural, and economic standing of women have probably caused the biggest changes in marriage over the last half-century, but there are other factors at work as well. And as we'll see in the chapters that follow, such changes are nothing new. Marriage is a relationship that has changed and evolved dramatically over time, more dramatically than most people probably realize. To put it simply, marriage as we know it today is far different from what it was in the past.

My question is, what do people believe about marriage today? And, more important, what do *Christian* people believe about marriage? Is there something that could be called a Christian marriage? Or maybe a Christian *view* of marriage?

In many cases, the people who came to my class brought with them very practical and specific concerns. Sometimes, from the questions they would ask, I could sense that they were asking about their own marriages. They wanted to know if there was something more they should be doing, if their own marriages could be better than they sometimes were. They were genuinely eager to know if the Bible taught something about marriage that they should be listening to.

"Under what circumstances," I could hear a few of them asking, "would it be okay for me to walk away from my marriage?"

My biggest surprise, as I taught the class, was how little Christian people really know about marriage. Most of us have assumptions and expectations, of course, but very few us, I began to see, have very many certainties about marriage. And clearly no certainties as far as a *Christian* marriage is concerned.

At one point during the ten-week series, a class member raised her hand and suggested that a vow renewal ceremony might be a good idea. I sensed almost immediate agreement from other members of the class and promised I would give it some thought.

My only previous experience with a vow renewal ceremony, one involving a large number of couples, had been a positive one.

It happened in the tiny Galilean village of Cana, in a church built where Jesus had been a guest at a marriage ceremony with his disciples and had turned water into wine. Of all the interesting places our tour group stopped in Israel, that particular one turned out to be one of the most memorable. I had anticipated and prepared for all of the other places we had visited, but I had no idea what would happen at this church until the bus stopped there. Our guide announced that Christian pilgrims, over the centuries, have renewed their vows on this site, and we could do so too, if we wanted. Then he abruptly turned things over to me.

Our tour group liked the guide's idea immediately.

I confess that I made the ceremony up as I went along, but something about it felt right. By the time we were finished, there wasn't a dry eye in that little church. And several years later, church members who made that trip with me still talk about our stop in Cana and our renewal of marriage vows as if it were the high point of our trip to the Holy Land.

To be honest, I had mixed feelings about this most recent request. I didn't want to offer married people something we weren't offering to single people, for example. It's important in church life to be fair and balanced in the programs we offer (an issue I'll return to in a later chapter). I also worried about how to make it an inclusive event, one to which every married person felt invited — not simply those who attended my class.

In the end I went along with the idea, but I had no way of knowing what would eventually happen.

On a Sunday night in February — the weekend of Valentine's Day, as it turned out — my church held its first vow renewal ceremony ever, and it made the front page of the newspaper on Monday morning. No one in town could remember anything quite like it. And my guess is that, after the newspaper coverage we received, several other pastors in the area will be experiencing intense lobbying to do something similar in their churches.

More than forty couples participated, all church members. Before the ceremony, we jammed into the choir room beneath the sanctuary, and I gave a few last-minute instructions. Some of the couples were dressed in formal clothes. One bride still fit into her wedding dress and wore it proudly. A couple of the men wore tuxedos, though probably not the ones they were married in. There was laughter and joking and even nervousness, altogether a feeling that I can't easily describe, though it was very much like the mood I see in brides and grooms before they're married in my church.

To me the mood said, "This is important, and even though we're having fun, we're taking this very, very seriously." As for my own feelings that night, I found myself deeply moved to be with members of my congregation on such an obviously important evening in their lives.

Some had taken their vows decades ago; some had said "I do" more recently. One couple had been married for sixty-two years, another for less than five. The rest of us were somewhere in between. All of us processed into the sanctuary that night while our children — and in some cases our grandchildren — looked on from the back of the church. Those who had been married the shortest length of time entered the sanctuary first. Those who had been married the longest came last, with the newly married couples looking to the back of the church as they entered — in effect, honoring those whose marriages had endured for so long.

The mood was electric. And tender.

The ceremony came almost word for word from the Presbyterian Book of Common Worship. I simply adapted the marriage rite for the occasion. When we came to the time for the exchange of vows, I asked couples to stand right where they were — in the pews — to face each other. The scene was unlike anything else that I've witnessed at my church.

Together we repeated the words to the traditional wedding vows — first the men, then the women. I held hands with my own wife, at the front of the church, as I led everyone through the vows. After twenty years of officiating at wedding ceremonies, I knew the words from memory:

> I, Doug, take you, Susan,
> to be my wife.
> And I promise, before God and these witnesses,
> to be your loving and faithful husband,
> in plenty and in want,
> in joy and in sorrow,
> in sickness and in health,
> as long as we both shall live.

Afterward I looked around and saw smiles and tears, sometimes both on the same faces. One couple told me they repeated their vows privately, on each anniversary, though they had never done it in the church and never with such a large group of people. But most of these couples had never renewed their vows before. Clearly, the act of renewing promises meant something profound to everyone who participated. No one would soon forget what we had done together.

What I didn't see, remarkably enough, were any looks of boredom, as though participants were eager for our little ceremony to be over. Everyone seemed to be fully present and fully engaged in what was happening. What makes that remarkable — to me — is that I frequently see looks of boredom on the faces of people at weddings, even those in the wedding parties. Often it's almost as though the wedding ceremony is a necessary — but unwelcome — preliminary to the main event, which of course is the reception. Although as a general rule I don't attend many receptions, my impression is that more and more guests skip the ceremony altogether and go directly to the reception.

On this particular night, the looks on the faces of those who participated said something different. Couples had agreed together about whether or not they wanted to be a part of this event and what their participation might mean. They had talked together about the significance of participating with family and friends looking on. And most couples had spent time in anticipation, getting ready. But most important, they had allowed themselves to focus on the words they were speaking to each other.

A few couples rather sheepishly confessed to me afterward that they hadn't really paid much attention to the promises they made the first time, which made the second time all the more meaningful. I found these confessions remarkable, given the far-reaching nature of the promises couples are expected to make at a wedding ceremony, but I now know that the experience isn't unusual.

Following the vow renewal ceremony, the group moved into the church's living room for a brief reception, where a designated best man and maid of honor made toasts, sometimes funny, sometimes tearful. Around the room, arranged on tables, were wedding photos of most of the couples who had participated in the ceremony. Most of us, it was clear, had changed considerably from the day we were married. We were older, and our hairstyles had changed — dare I say for the better? But what hadn't changed was the desire to be married to the other person in the photograph.

As one man said to the newspaper reporter after the ceremony, "Making the promise was even more meaningful this time because I knew what I was getting myself into." I think we all knew what he meant.

The entire event lasted for a little over an hour. But the effects still linger.

For several weeks afterward I reflected on all that had happened and worked hard to make sense of it, hoping to understand the level of interest and the depth of participation in a particular way.

As with most marriage ceremonies, our vow renewal ceremony evoked a wide range of feelings, all the way from joy to sadness. They joy came from the success, on a deep level, of the event. I also felt a sense of sadness — though perhaps for a different reason than my fellow participants. As I had looked around the sanctuary the night of the ceremony, I could easily imagine that some of those marriages would end during the coming year. Over the years I have come to see that marriage is a fragile thing, more so than people sometimes want to admit. Among the people who gathered to renew their vows, the sudden death of a partner or an unexpected divorce could conceivably bring one or more of those marriages to an end.

When I thought about the overall impact of the class, I was struck by a number of things. What I felt most strongly, though, was a confirmation of something I had suspected all along: Christian people want answers to their questions.

They wonder if it's possible for their faith to speak words of assurance and hope and encouragement about marriage to people like themselves who are already married. They wonder what their faith says to people like their children and grandchildren, who often have very different ideas about what marriage is. And they wonder, as I did, what it is exactly that Christians believe about marriage.

I had been thinking about marriage for a long time. And the questions that class members asked, together with some of my own, pushed me to find answers.

And that's how I came to write this book.

What Is a Christian View of Marriage?
An Introduction

In the deepest sense, marriage is inescapably religious. . . . When I say "I do" to my beloved — even if it's not in church and even if I don't feel a bit religious about what I am saying — I am necessarily declaring myself on matters of supreme and, therefore, religious importance.

David Blankenhorn, *Christianity Today*

I am a pastor, and the church I serve is a large, mainline Protestant church. I've been engaged in parish ministry for more than twenty years in three different churches.

No one could have prepared me for the huge amount of time I devote to marriage-related activities. I sometimes wonder why no one along the way thought to warn me. But the truth is, the time I give to marriage is far greater than I ever would have believed.

I prepare couples for marriage. I rehearse their ceremonies with them and deal with the seemingly endless questions about what is or is not permitted in the church before, during, and after the ceremony. I officiate at the ceremonies themselves, and then as an agent of the civil government I sign their marriage licenses for them.

8

I preach sermons about marriage too, not only at marriage ceremonies but also at other times of the year. In fact, by my estimate, I preach more sermons about marriage than about any other single subject. And I suspect I'm not the only pastor for whom this is true.

Beyond that, I work with married people on issues in their marriages and am expected to be something of an expert on marriage-related issues. I regularly refer couples to marriage counselors. I provide pastoral care to people who are at the end of their marriage relationships. And — this is relatively recent — I have been asked to bless same-sex covenant relationships and to have an opinion on the morality of those relationships.

If all of that weren't enough, I am married myself — and have been for more than twenty years.

To say that marriage and the issues surrounding marriage are a big part of my life and my ministry would be an understatement. But I haven't always had a very clear understanding of the Christian view of marriage.

In the first church I served after seminary, I was an associate pastor, and at least half of my job was calling on the sick and homebound members of the church. It was an older congregation — at least it was when I first began my ministry — and so there was a large number of people on our shut-in list.

According to my records, I officiated at about fifty funerals that first year, almost one per week — a disturbingly high average for any pastor, but certainly a frightening number for any first-year pastor.

Talk about a baptism by fire.

Early on, the senior pastor of the church told me that I would have to figure out for myself what I believed about death, the Christian view of death. Otherwise, he predicted, I wouldn't be able to do my job.

He was right. Very quickly I embraced the biblical promise of a resurrection to eternal life in a way I never had before, and that's the hope I proclaimed in my funeral sermons — and the

hope I clung to for my own sanity. Some days it was more difficult than others, but I always knew what I believed. Death is not
the end. We have hope in a life beyond death.

For some reason, however, I was never challenged to reach
that same level of clarity or rock-solid conviction on the subject
of marriage. I never wonder what I ought to say at a funeral, but
over the years I have wondered about what there is to say at a
wedding.

Don't get me wrong. I'm sure that my wedding sermons
have been biblically based and doctrinally sound. But there's
something about marriage that at times has felt vague and confusing to me.

Only in the last couple of years, especially as a consequence
of the reading and research I did for my adult education class on
marriage, have I started to experience the same kind of clarity
and conviction about marriage that I have long felt about death.

Most Christians who want answers to difficult questions turn
first to the Bible. Which is what I did when I prepared to teach
my adult class on marriage. I wanted to know what the Bible
teaches us about marriage.

What I found is that it doesn't teach us as much as we would
like.

The fact is, the Bible doesn't teach us all that much about
marriage, and considering how important marriage is to most
Christian people, that's surprising. To some people, I suspect, it's
also going to be disturbing. And yet, it's important to see that the
Bible contains very few guidelines or instructions about marriage.

When the Bible does mention marriage, often what it says
seems terribly confusing. Polygamy and arranged marriages, for
example, were accepted practices in the world that produced the
Bible. They aren't today.

Reread those wonderful old stories in Genesis about Abraham and Sarah, Isaac and Rebecca, Jacob and Rachel. Their understanding of marriage is startlingly different from ours today,

isn't it? It's safe to say that we wouldn't want our marriage relationships to look anything like theirs.

David's son Solomon, who "loved the LORD" (1 Kings 3:3), began his reign as the king of Israel by marrying the daughter of Pharaoh, king of Egypt. The marriage wasn't about love. It was instead a shrewd and calculated political move. During his reign, in fact, Solomon added seven hundred more foreign-born wives and three hundred concubines to his royal household, often as a way of extending or at least solidifying his kingdom. By the end of his life, "the LORD was angry with Solomon" (1 Kings 11:9), but not — it's important to note — because of his marital practices. God was angry with Solomon, the Bible tells us, because "his heart had turned away from the LORD." His foreign-born wives had something to do with that, of course, but the point is, much of the Old Testament seems to accept polygamy as a way of life.

Here's one of the surprising conclusions I came to early in my research: Anyone who looks to the Bible for marital role models will find few, if any, among the Old Testament heroes of faith.

But how can that be?

What has happened is that our understanding of marriage has changed between then and now, just as it continues to change today. Our understanding of marriage *always* seems to be evolving, as a matter of fact, usually in response to changes in the surrounding culture. For some people, of course, that in itself can be terribly confusing. How is it possible to find truths about marriage in the Bible when the culture that produced the Bible is so vastly different from our own? How is it possible to talk about a *biblical* view of marriage when the marriages described in the Bible are so vastly different from the kind of marriage we would find acceptable today?

I believe it *is* possible to describe a biblical view of marriage, but getting there is going to require taking a very careful, very thorough look at the Bible. My sense about the Bible is that it says both less and more than we sometimes think it does.

The Bible says *less* about marriage in the sense that there are very few places where it tells us exactly how to have a successful, satisfying, and God-honoring marriage. In fact, few of the passages in the Bible that we cherish for their commentary on love and commitment were written with marriage in mind. That's true even of those favorite verses from 1 Corinthians 13, which couples often ask to have read at their wedding ceremonies.

We might hope for something much more explicit and direct, but we aren't going to find it. To the disappointment of many, that's just not how the Bible is written.

To put it bluntly, marriage in the Old Testament — and to a certain extent in the New Testament as well — was largely an economic matter. Women were property. They had very few rights. For example, if a couple divorced and a financial settlement was required, the money wasn't paid to the woman, as it usually is in our culture. Concepts like alimony and maintenance were unknown in the ancient world. The financial settlement was paid to the woman's father — in order to appease him, because he was, after all, the woman's previous owner. A woman in those days was worth roughly fifty shekels of silver.

Today we're particularly interested in the romance of marriage. But the Bible has relatively little to say about that as well. In fact, for a thoroughly unromantic view of marriage, read the parts of Deuteronomy that regulate ancient marriage, especially 22:13-30.

So the Bible says less about marriage than we want it to.

But the Bible also says *more* about marriage than we might sometimes imagine. In this regard, it's helpful to remember that the Bible is a remarkable collection of different literary genres — history, poetry, prophecy, correspondence, and more. Within these different genres are surprisingly rich and suggestive insights about marriage. To find them, though, one must lift them carefully from their original settings, much like a trained archeologist lifts a piece of pottery from an excavation. It's sometimes hard work, I discovered, but the discoveries can be priceless. In undertaking this process, we'll find that the Bible has many valuable things to say about marriage — but we'll often find them in unexpected places.

Not all Christians are of the same mind about marriage. Those differences can be — and often are — confusing for Christian people, but I believe those differences can actually be illuminating. Looking at what Christians from other theological traditions believe about marriage may actually deepen and enrich our own views.

Many Christians today, including the millions worldwide who belong to the Roman Catholic Church, believe marriage is a sacrament. I think it's crucial for Protestant Christians to know what it means to call marriage a sacrament, whether or not we happen to agree with those who do.

If marriage isn't a sacrament, though, what is it?

In the theological tradition I embrace, the Reformed tradition, which traces its origins to sixteenth-century Reformers like John Calvin, marriage isn't a sacrament. We try to be quite clear about that. What we in our tradition emphasize instead is that marriage is a covenant. But what's a covenant?

Few people today — even those in my own church, I learned — seem to know exactly what a covenant is or how it informs our understanding of marriage. I think Christian people, particularly those in my own tradition, should know what a covenant is and what the Bible teaches us about covenants.

In the chapters that follow, I plan to describe how entering into marriage in a covenantal way provides marriage with a deep and strong foundation. Covenant also provides an illuminating way to think about marriage. On a practical level, I'll offer suggestions to couples on negotiating a marriage covenant. I'll even include a sample covenant that one couple wrote for their own marriage and read to family and friends at their wedding ceremony.

But — and here's an insight that has guided me in the writing of this book — I've come to see that covenant by itself isn't enough. Theologically, covenant just isn't adequate to explain all that marriage is or can be. Covenant, an exceedingly important biblical term, just can't hold all the weight that we would like it to. Christian people should know what a covenant is, as I've said,

13

and how it applies to marriage, but I believe that a more vital and compelling way to think about marriage is to think about it sacramentally.

Covenant may describe well enough the *foundation* of our marriage relationships, but sacrament, I have come to see, describes the *quality* of that relationship.

That's why I plan to start with a careful look at both covenant and sacrament. What I'm after is a theology of marriage, and though I plan to address matters like love, sex, and power as they relate to marriage, my immediate concern is to say what Christians believe about marriage.

Let me be as clear as I can about what I'm *not* planning to do in this book.

I'm a pastor, as I mentioned. I'm not a therapist. I've had some excellent training along the way in listening skills, and I think I know when to refer a couple for marriage counseling. But my strength is definitely not on the therapeutic side of marriage. I don't do marriage counseling, and in general I think pastors shouldn't attempt to be marriage counselors. Very few of us have adequate training, and very few of us receive any kind of supervision. In my experience, even gifted pastors who have the best of intentions can quickly find themselves in over their heads when they attempt to be counselors.

What I plan to do here is what I do Sunday after Sunday from the pulpit at my church — apply biblical truths to everyday life. In other words, this book is more about theology than psychology. My calling, as I understand it, is to help people make the connection between their faith and their lives.

So this isn't a book for people who want help with specific problems in their own marriages. This book, more than anything, is intended to be a theology of marriage. It's for Christian people who want to read and reflect about the meaning of their own marriages. It's for couples who are thinking about getting married and wondering what marriage really is. It's for study groups — both singles and couples — who want to discuss together how their faith informs and shapes marriage. And finally, it's for pastors who find themselves in the same awkward position I was once in — a marriage professional with little or no theological framework from which to operate.

I've also come to the conclusion, reluctantly, that I can't say as much as I would like about same-sex partnerships or unions.

It's not as though something shouldn't be said. Whether or not we want the conversation, our culture is prodding Christian people to say what we believe. Both city and state governments, for example, are beginning to pass laws governing domestic partnerships. Corporations too are beginning to extend health and pension benefits to same-sex partners. Christian people are in need of wise biblical and theological thinking on this subject.

In the adult education course I taught about marriage, I included a class on same-sex partnerships — one hour-long session. I realized that class members were strongly interested in this particular topic, just as they were in the others. But I realized a few other things as well. First, the topic is a large and complex one. I'm afraid that a single chapter, standing alongside other chapters on love, power, and divorce, for example, wouldn't begin to do justice to the topic. There isn't a great deal of biblical material about homosexuality, but what there is requires thoughtful examination. Second, the topic is emotionally charged — not just at my church, but in many American churches. And because the topic is so charged, because polarization happens just about every time it's discussed, I'm afraid that exploration of the topic in this context could mean that the insights into marriage I want to offer might be lost or obscured. Perhaps it will suffice here to say that the issue of same-sex relationships requires more prayerful and careful consideration by the church and its members.

The question I started with was this: What is it that Christians believe about marriage? My reading and research have led me on an exciting journey as I looked for answers to that question.

In one of my more modest bits of research, I went to Amazon.com, the well-known Internet bookseller, just to see what books were already available on marriage. To my surprise — and initial chagrin — I found that there were over a hundred thousand titles about marriage alone.

So I refined my search to *Christian* marriage, and even then I had to scroll through thousands of titles. Reading some of those titles was instructive. And here are some of the conclusions I came to.

First, the vast majority of books about Christian marriage are written today from a therapeutic point of view. In other words, they're about the psychology of marriage, not the theology of marriage. With very few exceptions, the titles I saw were about ways to save or improve marriages.

What the titles — and the sheer number of volumes — suggest to me is that our marriages are very important to us. We're looking hard for ways to make our marriages better. We want them to be as good as they can possibly be.

While I found many how-to books in my research, what I didn't find was a book about marriage that asks more basic questions. Suggestions for improving the communication between my wife and me are always welcome. It's not as though I don't need help in that area. But that's not what I was looking for. I might have been happy with a chapter here or there on *why* I should work harder at communicating with my wife, but I found little or none of that emphasis.

In fact, in all my research I came across only a handful of titles that attempted to answer some of the questions I've been raising in this introduction. And who wrote these books prompted my second conclusion: Interestingly (according to my rather unscientific research methods), the people who seem to be most concerned about the biblical and theological questions surrounding marriage are Roman Catholics.

Surprised? At first so was I.

Some of the most intriguing titles about Christian marriage — and how faith informs marriage — seem to have been written by Catholic authors. Why is this the case? The complete answer is probably beyond the scope of this book. But a big part of the answer is probably that the Roman Catholic Church has always insisted on a particular theological view of marriage, as we'll see in another chapter, and that view by its nature has required careful explanation and justification.

My findings were interesting. And they begged the question: What do people *from my own tradition* believe about marriage? What does our virtual silence about the subject mean?

At a deeper level, how do we know when marriage is good? What should we know before we get married? What should we know before we end a marriage? How important are love and sex to sustaining marriage? Does our tradition speak to that? How significant is spiritual compatibility? And what about authority and power issues within marriage? What does the Bible say about who's in charge?

By exploring these and other questions, I hope to initiate a conversation on a subject that I believe has been neglected, at least among Protestant Christians. I don't expect to exhaust every topic or say everything that can be said about the topics I address. This book is for Christian people like the ones in my own congregation, who helped me get started by asking the right questions. It's not a scholarly treatment of the subject — though I happen to think there's a need for just such a book. My work would certainly have been easier if I could have found one. But until that book appears, my hope is to make a start in the best possible place for theological questions to emerge — in the lives of real people, with real questions about real marriages.

I mentioned that I've been married for more than twenty years. I think that's a significant detail. I write this book from the perspective of a person who enjoys being married and who is an enthusiastic proponent of marriage. I certainly don't claim to know everything about marriage, but I do feel confident that I know enough to start a thoughtful conversation about it.

In this conversation, it was important to me to address the topic of singleness. I wanted to explore the connections that exist between married people and single people — connections that exist but often aren't properly acknowledged or appreciated. Because at this point I've lived more of my life as a married person than as a single person, I enlisted the help of several of my friends who are single, and I'm very grateful for their contributions. The subject of singleness seems particularly important now, given the fact that most people wait longer to get married than they used to, and given the sad fact that many marriages today end in divorce, thus turning couples into single people again.

I've done my best to acknowledge the perspective I have on marriage, and my hope is that everyone — married and single — will find their questions and concerns about marriage addressed here.

My wife, Susan, is an attorney who practices divorce law. That's a significant detail as well. She's also a licensed divorce mediator and for many reasons would prefer to mediate rather than litigate the dissolution of a marriage, but either way her job is to shepherd people through the final stages of their marriages. She says she likes her work best when she's able to see it in just this way, as her ministry.

Her experience over the years has shaped my thinking. I don't know Susan's clients, and for professional and ethical reasons it's a good idea for me not to know them. But I'm aware that the people Susan sees are hurting people. They don't come to the decision to end a marriage lightly. For most if not all of them, it's the single most difficult decision that they've ever made.

I mention this for several reasons, but the most important is this: People, especially Christian people, take marriage seriously. In spite of the perception that people today just walk out of their marriages at the first sign of trouble, Susan's experience — and mine too — tells me something very different.

Divorce rates are high, but not because marriage is taken lightly. The issue, as we'll see, is deeper than how easy it is today to get divorced. Frankly, I'm not convinced that divorces are all that easy, but that's another subject to which I'll return. The deeper issue is about marriage itself — what we believe about it and what we expect from it.

Here's my observation about marriage and divorce, based on my pastoral experience of more than twenty years: No one I know has ever entered a marriage lightly — or for that matter has ever left it lightly. Divorce is excruciatingly difficult. The pain of ending a marriage is such that, unless you've done it, you can't imagine just how difficult it is.

We all know, of course, about some well-publicized exceptions to my experience, often involving Hollywood celebrities or sports stars. But in general my experience tells me that marriage is important to us. We take it seriously. We enter into it with the best of intentions. And if we leave it, we do so with a profound sense of regret, often a feeling that we carry around for years.

Most married people want their marriages to be as good as they can possibly be. And my sense is that our expectations for marriage are actually higher today than they were years ago.

What should Christian women and men expect from a marriage? Do the Bible and our theological tradition give us some clues?

I believe they do.

A couple I know were married for thirty-five years. When they had been married for thirty-three years, the husband was diagnosed with a serious form of cancer, one with a very low survival rate. The last two years of their marriage were difficult ones. Slowly, he became weaker, less able to take care of himself. Increasingly, she became his primary caregiver. Toward the end, she both fed and bathed him.

After he died, I was able to spend a great deal of time with her, listening as she spoke about the feelings she had in response to his death. I'm sure she gave more to me in terms of my understanding of marriage than I was able to give to her in terms of pastoral care. As I expected, she had feelings of loneliness that in the early stages of her grief were intense and nearly overwhelming at times. These feelings were understandable after thirty-five years of almost constant companionship.

What moved me most was when she described the feeling

that she had lost the only other person who had shared and understood the last thirty-five years of their life together. Most of what they had experienced together was now her memory alone. There was no one else to discuss it with, no other person who understood, and no other person who could laugh and cry over all that had happened during the course of their marriage.

She was now alone, she told me, in more ways than she could possibly have imagined.

Marriages, especially marriages like this one that endure for thirty years or more, have a mysterious and unexplainable quality about them. It has to do with companionship, to be sure, but it's obviously much more than that. There are deep personal bonds — emotional, physical, and spiritual. When marriage is good, when it's deeply and mutually satisfying, and when it endures over many years, these bonds are nearly impossible to describe. But they're there.

We believe that this is what God intended for us, that God gave us to each other for this purpose. The book of Genesis calls it becoming "one flesh." In the chapter on marriage as a sacrament, I'll call it "a visible sign of God's grace." The rite I use at wedding ceremonies calls it "a holy mystery." This is the language of metaphor and of poetry, but it's the best we have.

Not all of us get to experience marriage at this level, I know. But Christians believe that this is what God intends for us, that this is what God made possible for us in creation.

This, I believe, is sacramental marriage, and in the chapters that follow I plan to describe what this marriage looks like.

Covenants and Covenant Marriages

> *Contracts deal with things; covenants deal with people. Contracts engage the services of people; covenants engage persons. Contracts are made for a stipulated period of time; covenants are forever. Contracts can be broken, with material loss to the contracting parties; covenants cannot be broken, but if violated, they result in personal loss and broken hearts.*

> Paul Palmer

If I had to choose a single word that best describes what Christians believe about marriage, I would choose the word "covenant." No other word even comes close in importance. Covenant is the very foundation of the Christian understanding of marriage. Anyone writing a theology of marriage would almost certainly begin with the word "covenant."

What makes an understanding of covenant all the more important, I believe, is that every Christian tradition makes essentially the same claim — that marriage is, at its core, a covenant.

Catholic, Protestant, Orthodox — *all* branches of the faith seem to agree, remarkably enough, on this one truth. Tell me, how often does that happen? These traditions may come to different conclusions about the implications of covenant — and we'll explore a couple of them — but on this one truth they are in agreement.

But what *is* a covenant? Do you know?

I asked that question in my adult education class on marriage, and participants were mostly stumped. We filled a page or two of newsprint with words that generally describe covenant, words like "promise" and "agreement," but no one was willing to offer a concise definition of the word.

This concerned me, because it's hard to imagine a more basic word in our Bible vocabulary. It would be nearly impossible to read the Old Testament, in particular, without at least an acquaintance with the word and its meaning.

I had always thought of "covenant" as a biblical and theological word, rooted in those wonderful stories of the Old Testament about Noah and Abraham, and so when I first read about its use in state laws about marriage, I was surprised, to say the least. I wondered if those laws could possibly mean the same thing that Christians do.

According to the biblical record, God is a covenant-maker. Almost from the beginning, God entered into covenants with human beings, agreements often made in dramatic and startling ceremonies. Most Christian people have heard these stories over the years, but my sense is that we seldom put them together in such a way that they form a pattern or story that makes sense to us.

In many ways the entire Bible is one long story about God's covenant. And Christian people today are children of that covenant. We are heirs, as the Apostle Paul puts it, of all the promises that we read about in Scripture.

A covenant, it's important for us to see, is different from a contract. A contract, according to its legal definition, is an agreement between two parties in which they assent to do (or not do) a certain thing. Technically, a contract requires an offer, an acceptance of that offer, and then something usually referred to as consideration, which is traditional legal language for the benefit received.

When you think about it, this definition fits a lot of marriages.

Many — if not most — marriages today are, in fact, legal contracts: there are an offer or a proposal (of marriage), an acceptance (the engagement), and a consideration (lifelong bliss, I suppose). Over the centuries, governments have played an important role in enforcing and regulating the contracts that their citizens enter into, including marriage contracts.

For a marriage to be more than a contract, we would say that there must be something more. And for Christians this "something more" is rooted in the biblical understanding of covenant.

Covenants in Scripture

The Old Testament stories about covenants God makes with people ordinarily have two elements — a promise and a sign.

One of the first covenants the Bible describes is between God and Noah (Gen. 9:8-17). God said, "I am establishing my covenant with you and your descendants after you, and with every living creature that is with you . . . as many as came out of the ark." Even the animals, it's interesting to see, are included in this particular covenant! And as you probably recall from the story, the "bow in the clouds" — the rainbow — was a sign of that covenant, reminding God always of the promise made to Noah.

Later, God made a covenant with Abraham when he was ninety-nine years old (Gen. 17:1-22). God said, "I will establish my covenant between me and you, and your offspring after you throughout their generations, for an everlasting covenant, to be God to you and to your offspring after you." Here the emphasis is clearly on the enduring quality of the covenant. This time circumcision was the sign, an indelible reminder of Abraham's new identity. Abraham and his descendants (his *male* descendants) would never have to wonder who they were or whose they were!

Still later, God made a covenant with David (2 Sam. 7:4-29), and this one in many ways is even more touching and personal than the previous ones because God puts it in warm, personal terms. He promises to take care of Israel and David — and even promises to care for David's son after David dies. God says to the prophet Nathan, "I will be a father to him [meaning Solomon], and he shall be a son to me." It was Nathan's task to convey those tender words. No specific sign is mentioned with this covenant, though it may well be found in the relationship itself.

Finally, in the New Testament, Jesus established a covenant at the Last Supper with his disciples (Luke 22:19-20): "Then he took a loaf of bread, and when he had given thanks, he broke it and gave it to them, saying, 'This is my body, which is given for you. . . .' And he did the same with the cup after supper, saying, 'This cup that is poured out for you is the new covenant in my blood.'" Here the sign and the promise are clearly made one. Jesus' body and blood are for us both the sign and the promise.

The idea of covenant didn't begin with Israel. As with many elements of their life together, the people of Israel borrowed the idea of covenant from their neighbors and then gave it new meaning.

Covenants in the ancient world were established, typically, when the king of a conquering nation gave the terms or conditions for peace to a conquered nation. Ordinarily there was a covenant ceremony too, in which the newly conquered vassal promised to fulfill the terms of the covenant or face an unpleasant consequence. Read Genesis 15:7-19, where *God* ceremonially accepts the consequences if the covenant promises are not kept.

Covenants in the ancient world were imposed on conquered peoples, and Israel understood that God initiated the covenant with them. But God's covenant with Israel was different in both motive and character. God called the people into relationship and promised them identity, security, long life, land, and much more. God required only faithfulness in return.

God was interested, always and only, in an exclusive relationship. "I will be your God, and you will be my people." That's a constant refrain in Old Testament stories. And as you know from your reading of the Old Testament, faithfulness was a nearly impossible promise for the people to keep. But God did — and does — remain faithful.

When Christians talk about covenants today, these are the stories that ought to come to our minds. Covenant talk is impossible without remembering God and God's promises. The Bible doesn't give us a definition of covenant; it tells us stories. And from those stories it's clear that covenants are more than contracts. They are promises or agreements, of course, but they're more than that. Covenants have a spiritual dimension. Not only is God a partner in biblical covenants, but covenants are binding at a deeper, more profound level than contracts ever could be. Covenants, biblical covenants, involve us at the deepest level of our beings.

And that's true of covenant marriage as well.

The Old Testament prophet Hosea was the first, as far as we know, to make the explicit connection between God's covenant with the people of Israel and marriage. The idea of marriage as sacred was not new to people of the ancient world, but marriage as a covenant relationship was. It had certainly never been spelled out in quite this way.

Hosea's story can be a difficult one to read and understand. It's hard to imagine, for example, a couples' Bible-study group choosing to focus on this particular book as a way of reflecting together about marriage. On the other hand, the book of Hosea is important, and I wish more Christians were familiar with it.

In the eighth century B.C., God told Hosea to find a wife, and told him ahead of time that his wife would be unfaithful. She would bear several children, God informed him, and some of them would be fathered by other men.

It's hard to understand fully, except perhaps as an astonishing act of faithfulness, but Hosea married Gomer even though he knew in advance the outcome of this relationship. Subsequently, Hosea's relationship with Gomer, her adultery, and their children became a living, prophetic witness to Israel. The prophets often used object lessons to make their point, but here was a case where Hosea's marriage became a living symbol of the strained relationship between God and the people of Israel.

The book of Hosea is a love story — tragic at certain times and unbelievably tender at others. Mostly it is the story of God's love for the people and their unfaithful response. God's love was steadfast and his commitment unbroken, but his history with Israel, like Hosea's and Gomer's history, included one episode of unfaithfulness after another.

What's important for us to see here is the connection that Hosea has made between covenant and marriage. Marriage is a relationship that God calls us to, and it is to be characterized by love, faithfulness, and forgiveness. Even when the terms of the covenant are broken, there is the implied sense that the covenant itself can remain intact.

Biblical covenants are unconditional. That's an important point.

Promises of fidelity can be found in other places in the Bible. One of my personal favorites doesn't refer to a marriage relationship, but the far-reaching nature of the promise makes it a fitting story to read at any marriage ceremony. In fact, I wish more couples wanted to read these words at their wedding ceremonies.

In the Old Testament book of Ruth, Naomi's sons die in a foreign land and leave widows there. Deciding that her best hope for the future is in Israel, Naomi makes plans to return to her native land, only to find that Ruth, one of her daughters-in-law, wants to go with her. Ruth's words of fidelity are among the most beautiful in all of Scripture, and once again they are to be understood biblically as an example of God's faithfulness. In other words, what Ruth expresses in these verses is essentially what God demonstrates to the people of Israel throughout the Old Testament.

At first Naomi urges Ruth to remain among her own people and find a new husband from among them. But to her mother-in-law Ruth says,

"Do not press me to leave you
　　or to turn back from following you!
Where you go, I will go;
　　where you lodge, I will lodge;
your people shall be my people,
　　and your God my God.
Where you die, I will die —
　　there will I be buried.
May the Lord do thus and so to me,
　　and more as well,
if even death parts me from you!"

Now that's a promise!

What Is a Covenant Marriage?

Can we as Christians take the biblical background about covenant, along with the examples of Hosea and Ruth, and fashion all of it into a coherent statement about marriage today? I think so. As I see it, the statement has four major components.

First, in a covenant marriage we say that God takes the initiative.

That's fundamental to the very nature of covenants, and it's a constant theme of the Bible. God calls or invites people into relationship. Human beings, we believe, were created to be in relationship — not just with God but with each other.

More than that, God desires *men and women* to be in relationship with each other. Marriage was God's idea.

In the first creation story, found in Genesis 1–2, there is the remarkable suggestion that men and women together make up the image of God. Not men alone. Not women alone. But together. "In the image of God," we read, "he created them; male and female he created them" (Gen. 1:27).

In the second creation story, found in Genesis 2, Adam's life

27

is not complete until God provides a partner. There we read that God gave Adam and Eve to each other (2:18).

And the key is that — in covenant terms — God is going to be a partner in the relationship. By nature, God is always calling, inviting, initiating, providing for, and even establishing the terms and conditions of our relationships.

Second, in a covenant marriage, change and growth are both anticipated and accepted.

Partners in a marriage do change over time, as anyone who has ever been married knows. Furthermore, human beings don't grow and evolve at the same rate. I sometimes wish we did, but we don't. And in a covenant marriage, the expectation is that partners will change and grow at different times, but will adapt together, that they'll make it possible for each other.

Put another way, change itself is not a sufficient basis for the dissolution of the marriage relationship. Where the marriage agreement is based on a legal contract, of course, change and growth might well be problematic and can often lead to a voiding of the contract — or at the very least point out the need to renegotiate a new contract.

Not so with a covenant marriage.

A covenant by its very nature is elastic and flexible. Living as partners in a covenant implies having a dynamic, living, changing relationship. Forgiveness and acceptance are part of the package.

When God entered into a covenant with Abraham, God knew from the beginning that Abraham would sometimes break the terms of the covenant. Some of his behavior was touching and wise, but often his life was filled with mistakes and terrible misjudgments. If you don't remember Abraham's awful behavior, read the story again (Gen. 12–25). What's remarkable is not so much that Abraham was faithful to God (many times he wasn't); what's remarkable is that God was faithful to Abraham. The covenant endured.

Similarly, in a covenant marriage a couple knows from the

beginning that they will be imperfect partners. In my own marriage I knew that I would let Susan down, and I knew that she would let me down. We both knew what was going to happen before we entered the relationship.

And, by the grace of God, the covenant has endured.

Third, a covenant implies freedom.

Biblical covenants may not be voluntary. After all, God initiates them and calls us into them. But in every case God's covenants have the paradoxical quality of being life-giving and life-enhancing. God's promises to those who enter the covenant are simply staggering. Those who live outside God's covenant experience life as harsh, brutish, and short. Those who live inside discover that their lives are full, rich, and abundant.

Isn't that also the promise of covenant marriage?

By entering the marriage covenant, we are certainly limiting ourselves and restricting our freedoms. In an undeniable way, we are binding ourselves to another person. In fact, the Presbyterian marriage rite I use at one point asks bride and groom to "bind yourselves together as husband and wife." Another ceremony that I've used in the past calls marriage "a joyful burden."

But the promise of marriage, of *covenant* marriage, is that in the "binding" and in the "burden" there will — paradoxically — be freedom. I have more to say about how this works in my chapter on love, so for now let me make this brief point. In a long-term relationship characterized by trust and commitment — in other words, in a covenant relationship — partners are actually encouraged to discover who they are, to embrace new and unexpected gifts, and to let go of bad habits and vices. A covenant relationship offers us the freedom not only to grow but to be challenged.

Fourth, a marriage covenant, like its biblical counterparts, is intended to last.

A contract may spell out the duration of an agreement, but a covenant by its nature suggests something that is indissoluble, lifelong.

In every covenant that God made with Old Testament figures, there is a strong sense of forever. God makes the covenant "to us, and to our children, and to our children's children, throughout their generations." One of the great themes of the Bible, in fact, is God's steadfastness or unfailing love for us. Human beings may change, but God doesn't — at least not in his love for us. We can always count on that.

When couples make promises to each other, they typically promise faithfulness "as long as we both shall live." That's covenant language for "forever."

This leads me to my next question: What about *broken* covenants?

When Covenants Are Broken

What the Bible says about divorce is the subject of a later chapter, but for the purposes of this chapter, my question is how divorce fits with the idea of covenant. Given what we know about covenant as the Bible introduces it to us, is it even possible to think in terms of breaking a covenant? After all, God doesn't break covenants. How can we?

The reality is, even covenant marriages break down.

Is there a family anywhere today that hasn't known the pain of divorce? By now most people know the statistic that nearly half of all marriages will end in divorce. The rate is even higher for second marriages. Studies show that divorce is somewhat less frequent among Christian people — in other words, among couples who go to church together and actively practice their faith. But those same studies somewhat disturbingly show that the rate of divorce is actually higher than average among ordained clergy.

Regrettably, faith in God, even when both partners in a marriage embrace that faith, is not a predictor of a happy or lasting marriage. I wish it was, but it simply isn't. Divorce touches us all.

It's wise to acknowledge that all human beings, even those with the best of intentions, "fall short of the glory of God." The state of Louisiana, which has a new law for covenant marriage, seems to acknowledge this. Its provisions for divorce are based on covenant-breaking behaviors.

In my adult education class, I asked participants if they could guess what those behaviors were. They guessed all of them — and then some. Class members were adamant that, covenant or no covenant, there are actually many reasons to end a marriage — and probably several more than that new Louisiana law is willing to recognize.

In addition to adultery, the commission of certain felony crimes, abandonment, and various forms of abuse, class members offered a few more examples of covenant-breaking behaviors that I was hard-pressed to disagree with.

One person suggested "dishonesty." When I expressed some initial skepticism, she gave a heartbreaking example. The husband of one of her friends had, after several years of marriage and two children, announced that he was homosexual. He had known this before the marriage and had tried his best both to hide and to change his sexual orientation. He believed what some of his Christian friends had told him before he was married — that the "love of a good woman" would "cure" whatever desires he had for men. Evidently the love of his wife and his own efforts to change hadn't been enough. And the marriage ended.

Another person suggested that addictive behaviors would be covenant-breakers. And the more this person talked, the more I found myself agreeing. When you're married to an addict, this class member argued, it's as though your partner is being unfaithful. Whatever the addiction is — alcohol, drugs, gambling — it eventually becomes more important than the marriage itself. And often, though not always, effective treatment is elusive.

There were other suggestions as well, all good reasons why certain marriages should come to an end, and each one reminded me of the pain that people endure for the sake of their marriage commitments.

Are there other covenant-breaking behaviors that you would add to this list?

I agree that there's far too much divorce today. I grieve over the pain and suffering that people endure when they go through a divorce. I grieve over the effects these divorces have on the children who are involved. Over the years of my ministry I've listened to too many people, too many dear friends, as they've told me their stories of lost hopes and long-term disappointments.

In these situations I've found myself wishing I had known earlier that there was trouble, so that maybe I could have intervened, suggested a counselor, been more loving and attentive — done something more. I've wanted to take on some of the responsibility for these failed unions.

Faithful church members have a similar response when they hear of someone they know who is getting a divorce. "Isn't there something we can do?" they ask. "Isn't there something the church can do to support all of us in our marriages?" And the answer is, yes and no. There are speakers and programs and seminars. There are weekend retreats for couples. And for many couples these have been enormously helpful, sometimes even life-changing. I've heard their stories.

But not all marriages respond to these attempted cures.

So always, in the end, I come to the sad conclusion that these broken covenants were ultimately beyond my ability to mend and that they were beyond the ability of my church to mend. Something deeper was going on than my helpful ideas could address, something in the human heart.

Human beings make promises and then break them. We start out hopeful and wanting to do well, only to find that we can't make our relationships work. In spite of our deepest longings and most fervent prayers, sometimes our marriages don't last. Often we feel helpless in the face of what is happening to us.

Yes, something should be done. But I'm not convinced, as Louisiana legislators apparently are, that covenant marriage laws are the answer. I fear they will only make things worse. And my guess is that the new law will only make the end of some Louisiana marriages uglier and messier and more painful. Once a couple has reached the difficult conclusion that their marriage is irretrievably broken, waiting longer for the divorce to be granted is most likely not going to put the marriage back together.

I wish more couples would base their marriages on the biblical idea of covenant, but even that, I know, is not the full answer. Still, it would be a start. I wish more couples would enter into their commitments more deliberately, more thoughtfully, and with better preparation. I wish more couples would actually spend as much time planning their marriages as they do their receptions.

The Importance of Covenant-Making

How can couples avoid covenant-breaking? Perhaps by being more intentional in their covenant-making.

A few years ago I married a young couple named Laurie and Chip. I liked them immediately and told them so. They were thoughtful and sincere, as most couples are who come to me. Not only that, but they were very serious about their faith. And they wanted to be sure I was too! They were the first and only couple who have ever asked me how I came to believe in Jesus Christ as my Lord and Savior. And I found myself glad to tell them.

More than that, they expressed a desire to go beyond the few basic requirements our church has for couples getting ready to be married. And so we spent some time talking about how they might do that.

They told me that they had been reading Stephen Covey's book *The Seven Habits of Highly Effective People,* and they said they felt challenged by the book to write a mission statement for their marriage. They had already written personal mission statements, but they wanted to write one for the two of them. And then, as we talked about the idea further, they decided they would read their mission statement at their wedding ceremony. After the vows, they wanted to turn to their family and friends, read the statement, and then ask everyone to hold them accountable to what they had written. I was enthusiastic about their plan, and even more so when I saw the final version of their statement. They had done a wonderful job.

At the wedding they exchanged vows, and then, as planned, they read their mission statement. I won't soon forget the response. At first there was silence, as there is with anything new and somewhat startling. But then, when the sincerity and tenderness of the words became evident, the reaction of family and friends changed to smiles. I could see looks of pride on the faces of the parents and admiration on the faces of others.

We were witness to something truly unusual. So when Laurie and Chip finished reading their statement and asked for our promise of support, those of us who were in the congregation that day spontaneously said "Yes!" Who could have said no to a request like that?

Not all couples will want to do exactly what Laurie and Chip found the courage to do — nor will they want to do it in precisely the same way. For those of you who are interested, I've included (in an appendix) the mission statement that Laurie and Chip wrote — and also some suggestions for drafting a marriage covenant of your own. Even if you're already married, you may find the exercise helpful. You might be surprised to discover how many expectations in your marriage have never been verbalized. The making of a covenant is an opportunity to clearly express the hopes and dreams you have for your marriage — and also your expectations.

Conclusion

Having said all of that, I find something missing.

There's absolutely no doubt that covenant is an essential foundation for thinking about Christian marriage. As a matter of fact, it would be impossible to think of relationships from a biblical point of view *without* mentioning covenant. Every Christian couple who gets married enters into a covenant, and those who clarify the goals of their union, as Chip and Laurie did, are starting their relationship on solid ground.

And yet, I sense that there ought to be something more. How do you know, for example, if you have a good marriage? On what evidence would you make your judgment? If you're a married couple, is it enough to say that you've entered into a lifelong covenant initiated by God and designed for your mutual benefit? Maybe.

If your relationship is characterized by the biblical notion of covenant and all that covenant implies, you're building on a great foundation. But I find myself wanting to go beyond that, to say something about marriage that expresses all that I have discovered not only in my own marriage but also in so many other marriages I have known over the years.

Covenant takes us only so far.

Writing a marriage covenant can be a way for a couple to prepare for marriage, to clarify their hopes and expectations for marriage. And entering into the covenant of marriage, as church and Scripture understand it, provides a nurturing ground for a relationship to grow and deepen. But what about those happy, mutually satisfying relationships that endure for twenty, thirty, or forty years or more? To be around the people in those relationships is to feel blessed by them. I've come to see that covenant alone, as powerful as it is, can't account for them.

Something else — something more — is at work within them. Could it be called sacramental?

Sacraments and Sacramental Marriages

It is married life, much more than a marriage ceremony, that is both the prophetic symbol which proclaims and makes real and celebrates in representation the community between Christ and his Church and the life situation in which married men and women encounter Christ and God and grace.

Michael G. Lawler, *Secular Marriage, Christian Sacrament*

A few years ago a couple from my church decided to renew their vows on their fiftieth anniversary. They wanted to do it in the church sanctuary, and they wanted to invite the entire congregation to witness it and be a part of their celebration. When the day came, the church was filled with their children, grandchildren, and friends. More people came out on a Saturday afternoon for this event than I ever would have guessed.

After the exchange of vows, the seventy-something groom leaned over and whispered something to his seventy-something bride. He wanted his words to be private, I think, just between the two of them, but instead he spoke the words directly into my lapel microphone.

"Best promise I ever made," he said.

His words could be heard clearly throughout the church,

and when the congregation heard them and saw the surprised look on his face, they broke out in applause. That couple was — and still is — a visible sign of God's grace. Celebrating their fifty years of marriage with their church family was a way of making God's grace visible. By sharing with the rest of us, they gave us a wonderful gift, something for all of us to aspire to.

When marriage is a sacrament, as it is in the Catholic Church, the partners involved are said to be joined to Christ. Together husband and wife become a visible sign of God's grace.

Both Catholics and Protestants agree on at least that much — not that marriage is a sacrament, but on the definition of sacrament — that it involves a joining to Christ and a visible sign of God's grace.

What Christians have said over the years is that God meets us or becomes real to us in the sacraments. God is present in the sacraments in a way that God isn't present otherwise. And, significantly, God becomes real to us in a physical or tangible way — in the water of baptism, for example, or in the bread and wine of the Lord's Supper. That's the appeal of a sacrament. You can touch it, feel it, taste it, and even smell it. What Catholics and Protestants have always disagreed on is how, precisely, that happens.

To better understand this, we need to go back to the beginning, before there were Protestants and Catholics, before marriage was considered a sacrament.

Early Views of Marriage

It might surprise you to know that, in the beginning, the church took relatively little interest in marriage. Early in church history, celibacy was considered to be the preferred state. It was practically sacred. The Apostle Paul said as much in 1 Corinthians 7:1.

And marriage? Well, at the beginning it was all but ignored. As one writer puts it, "When asked, some priests might come by and say a blessing as a favor, just as they'd say a blessing over a child's first haircut." But that was about it.

Roman law spelled out most of the requirements for marriage, and, following the words of Jesus, most early Christians were content to "render unto Caesar" in matters pertaining to marriage.

Another seemingly small but critically important characteristic of marriage in the early days of the church is that marriage was typically announced rather than pronounced. I'll come back to this distinction later in the chapter, but for now it's important simply to recognize the difference between announced and pronounced marriages. Early on, couples — or rather, families — would simply *announce* that there was going to be a marriage, and the church took little notice.

At the beginning the church didn't *pronounce* a couple to be married. Church ceremonies to mark the beginning of a marriage were largely unknown, which may seem very strange today, when elaborate church weddings are the norm.

Centuries rolled by with virtually no change to this arrangement. But then something began to happen. Historians don't agree on all of the details, but what seems clear is that power became an issue. Slowly and unevenly, the church began to exert its control over Europe's social and political life, and this included the writing of laws pertaining to marriage, family, and sex. In 774, for example, the pope gave Charlemagne, emperor of the Holy Roman Empire, a set of writings that defined marriage and condemned all deviations from it.

But it wasn't until 1215, nearly twelve hundred years after Pentecost, that the Roman Catholic Church formally decreed marriage to be a sacrament — the least important one, to be sure, but a sacrament nonetheless. Equally important, the church established a systematic canon law for marriage — with a system of ecclesiastical courts to enforce it. These actions, it's important to see, profoundly shaped our understanding and practice of marriage until the last century.

In 1517 Martin Luther nailed his theses to the church door

in Wittenberg, and among his concerns were the Catholic Church's rules about marriage. In 1520, with increasing boldness, Luther publicly burned the canon law.

The battle had begun.

The most obvious issue that Protestants addressed was marriage as sacrament. Protestants believed that only those acts Jesus himself told us to perform could be sacraments — limiting the number to just two, baptism and the Lord's Supper. And because Jesus nowhere tells his followers to get married or offers explicit commands with regard to marriage, marriage couldn't be regarded as a sacrament. Reformers like Calvin were people of the Word, and the Word — in their view — didn't put marriage in the same category as baptism and the Lord's Supper.

And, centuries later, that's still the official Protestant viewpoint. Marriage has never qualified as a sacrament.

Even so, many of the couples who come to my church to be married, especially those who were raised Roman Catholic, are surprised to learn that marriage isn't a sacrament. After all, they ask, what is marriage if it isn't a sacrament?

Good question.

Marriage as Sacramental

For Protestants, marriage isn't a sacrament, but it is sacramental. Over the years it has become one of the rites of the church, and so it typically has the look and feel of a sacrament. There is certainly a tangible or physical reality about it, and further, we say that it is a sign of God's grace and presence.

Protestant Christians believe, as one liturgy puts it, that in marriage "husband and wife become one, just as Christ is one with the church." That's an extraordinary statement, and it has a sacramental ring to it, but what does it mean exactly?

It's difficult to say, but Christians believe something is supposed to happen in a marriage relationship that is deeply and profoundly mysterious. In the liturgy we refer to the marriage relationship as a "mystical union." In Genesis 2:24 the powerful description of this relationship is "one flesh." It is the deepest, most profound relationship that is possible to have with another human being, deeper in many ways than the relationship between parent and child.

Catholic theology actually has a helpful insight on this point. Marriage as sacrament, their theologians say, refers to the months and years of married life more than it does to the wedding ceremony. In other words, *God's grace becomes visible not only at the church as the vows are spoken, but during a lifetime of shared experiences.*

I once heard a Catholic theologian try to explain this point by telling an old joke. "When are two people married?" he asked. "Thirty years later!" he exclaimed after a brief pause. At the time I don't think I fully understood, but I'm beginning to.

Becoming a visible sign of God's grace takes time. It doesn't usually happen during the first week of marriage — or even during the first year of marriage. But as the months and years go by, as the marriage relationship deepens, as a couple draws together, something happens that can be described only in the language of poetry or metaphor. Marriage partners slowly but surely become "one flesh."

In a helpful book titled *Becoming Married,* Herbert Anderson and Robert Cotton Fite emphasize that becoming married takes time. It doesn't happen on the wedding day, they point out. In my chapter on family, I'll return to their insights about "leaving and cleaving," but for now it's enough to note what their book title suggests — that becoming married is for most people a process rather than a single event.

For some Christians, especially Protestant Christians, this may be a new insight into sacraments — or one we've never really considered before. We tend to think of a sacrament as something that happens at church. It happens during worship, lasts for a few minutes maybe, but not much more — and then it's over. In reality, though, a sacrament isn't something that's bound by a liturgy or a rite, so even though worship may come to end, a sacrament doesn't. A sacrament actually has an enduring quality.

Let's look at an example of how this works. When we're baptized, we sometimes say that we enter the covenant of baptism. In other words, a new and intimate relationship with God begins.

In some churches, mainly Roman Catholic churches, there are small bowls of water near the entrance to the sanctuary, and believers will sometimes dip their fingers into the water and then touch their fingertips to their foreheads as they enter. What they're doing, of course, is remembering their baptisms. They're remembering that they have entered into a relationship with God that endures over time, a relationship that can and must be renewed and refreshed.

In my church we don't have bowls of water at the entrance, but we often have opportunities in worship for people to renew their baptismal vows. Every time we celebrate the sacrament of baptism, we invite worshippers to remember their own baptisms. In fact, it's appropriate to renew our baptisms as often as every day.

The enduring nature of baptism is recognized at funerals, where we sometimes say in the liturgy that baptism is "complete in death." What we mean is that we enter a lifelong relationship at the moment of our baptisms and that this relationship continues and develops over time. At death, the relationship doesn't end; it's transformed.

It's important to see as well that sacraments aren't passive events. One of the things we're asked to do in a sacrament is to remember. In baptism we remember our identity as children of God. In the Lord's Supper we remember the sacrifice that Christ made on our behalf. In marriage — to think sacramentally about it — we remember the call to relationship. God desires that we have a partner for life, one who will be bone of our bones and flesh of our flesh.

If we consider marriage in a sacramental way, then the wedding is only the beginning of a relationship that can be expected to endure and grow. What happens is that over time God's grace becomes visible in the marriage relationship. It becomes visible and real to the married couple, of course, but in a wonderful way

41

it also becomes visible to the people who are touched by the relationship, to family and friends, to neighbors and fellow church members.

At most wedding ceremonies, I use a prayer from the marriage rite that seems to acknowledge this sacramental dimension of their life together:

> Make their life together
> a sign of Christ's love
> to this sinful and broken world,
> that unity may overcome estrangement,
> forgiveness heal guilt,
> and joy conquer despair.

To me that's a description of how God's grace works in a sacramental way. In a marriage that has a sacramental quality, everyone around it sees in it "a sign of Christ's love."

Changing Times, Changing Unions

One more small but important bit of history is relevant here.

Something else changed during the Reformation, and Christian people should know what it was. As usual, the smallest changes sometimes have the biggest consequences. Not only did Protestants reject the idea that marriage was a sacrament, but they also changed the very definition of marriage. And with this change in definition, a social revolution began.

With the Protestant Reformation of the sixteenth century, marriage went from being something that was *announced* to something that was *pronounced* — in other words, from something privately made to something publicly bestowed.

Protestants instituted several requirements that usually (depending on the region in Europe) had to be observed. A marriage had to involve a public ceremony presided over by a priest and attended by witnesses. The couple being married had to obtain parental consent (up to age twenty-one or even, in some places, twenty-five). And the marriage had to be entered in a public register of marriages.

Even the Roman Catholic Church, stung by Protestant criticism of its practices, eventually went along with these changes. In 1563 the Council of Trent decreed that a marriage not publicly performed in front of the parish priest was invalid.

But no Protestant group had the civil authority to bestow public recognition on a wedding, and Protestants weren't prepared to wait a thousand years, as the Catholic Church had, in order to build that power. So they handed it off to the local government.

And here is where the state first began to take such a strong interest in marriage, a far stronger interest than even the Romans had. Slowly at first, but later with great enthusiasm, civil governments relished this new power. Governments began to make rules about who could and who couldn't be married; they set the legal age for marriage; and they started to establish reasons for the dissolution of marriages.

Why make such an issue of the seemingly subtle difference between announced and pronounced marriages? Because, very simply, I think the difference is at the root of so many of our marriage controversies today.

In 1998 the mayor of New York, Rudolph Giuliani, proposed "domestic partnership" legislation to the New York City Council that would make unmarried co-habiting couples, both heterosexual and homosexual, the legal equal of married couples in a wide range of matters, from housing to death benefits to city contracts. Similar legislation has already been passed in San Francisco, and other cities are now considering the change as well.

The Roman Catholic Archbishop of New York, the late John Cardinal O'Connor, objected to Giuliani's proposal, as did other religious leaders, but no one should have been surprised by it.

For nearly five hundred years the civil government has been making all the rules about marriage, including what constitutes a marriage. This was a role the church — Roman Catholic and

Protestant — urged the civil government to take. And now that the church is no longer the powerful institution it once was, no one should be surprised that the civil government is moving to act in what it believes to be its own political interest.

But there's more at stake here.

The growing number of couples who choose to live together before marriage are a challenge not only to institutions such as the church and civil government. They're a challenge to long-established patterns of thinking, such as when marriage begins and who may be married.

Centuries ago, marriage began whenever a couple privately acknowledged that they were a couple. Private consent was all that was necessary. In Roman law, all a couple had to do to be considered married was to "regard each other as man and wife and behave accordingly." The Romans never quite defined what "behave accordingly" meant, but they knew it when they saw it.

Not all couples who live together would agree that they are married, even in a very limited sense. Sometimes, as a matter of fact, couples begin to live together and are quite emphatic that they're *not* married and that they have no plans to be married, at least not in the way our culture currently defines marriage. And yet, in just about every situation I know of, there is nevertheless the feeling of an announced partnership, even in those cases where the level of commitment is relatively low.

Couples of all age groups and income levels are living together, and according to recent surveys they are doing so in unprecedented numbers. This should be news to no one.

How Can Christians Respond?

At a recent clergy gathering, I sat at a table where everyone present — representing several different denominations as well as different regions of the country — said the norm was to marry couples who had been living together, many for a considerable period of time. If we refused to officiate at these weddings, we guessed that there would be very few — if any — weddings at our churches.

How are people of faith to understand what's happening around us?

The issue is a complicated one, and it's far more complicated than some have been willing to admit. Certainly the confusion many feel is undeniable.

Parents with children who are now young adults sometimes come to see me to ask for help in dealing with a child's live-in partner. They don't agree with the living situation, they say, but they don't want to threaten or end the relationship with their child, either. "What's the right thing to do?" they ask.

Similarly, I have spoken with people my own age whose widowed or divorced parents have live-in partners. The situation, they say, has left them with more questions than answers. They're perplexed by their parents' behavior when they remember how they were raised. And they're not sure what to tell their children about grandpa's or grandma's living situation. "What's happening?" they ask.

The honest — though not wholly satisfying — answer is that we're living in a time of social revolution. Living arrangements and patterns that were taboo for the last several hundred years are, quite simply, now accepted.

One possible explanation for the social changes we're seeing is a slow decline in the practice of pronounced marriages, along with a gradual acceptance of the practice of announced marriages. My sense about the living-together phenomenon is that our culture is making a return to the past — the *distant* past.

Many couples today simply begin to live together as couples, without waiting for or even wanting the church's blessing. To paraphrase the old Roman law, they are regarding each other as man and wife and behaving accordingly, even when they claim they're not.

Whether or not the church and the state regard those relationships as marriages, in most cases that seems to be exactly what they are. They are marriages in all but official recognition.

And I have no doubt that there are among them relationships of deep love, devotion, and commitment. Most of us, as a matter of fact, know people who have been in long-term, committed relationships where official recognition is sometimes planned, sometimes not.

In recent years the church has struggled with the morality of these relationships. In my own denomination, the Presbyterian Church (U.S.A.), our highest governing body, the General Assembly, has established new guidelines for ordination that specifically address these social changes. According to the new rules, known popularly as "the fidelity and chastity amendment," people who are not married may not hold an office in the church unless they are living in chastity.

Other denominations are wrestling with the same issues and proposing similar guidelines. It's a profoundly difficult time for the church.

I found it interesting to discover in my research that Karl Barth, one of the most important theologians of the last century, complained at one point in his *Church Dogmatics* about *how* these social changes were being addressed. Both Catholics and Protestants, he wrote, tend to deal with marriage in legal or constitutional ways rather than theological ones. It's time, he said, for some good theological thinking about marriage.

That was fifty years ago.

This takes us back to the question I asked at the beginning of this book: What is it that Christians believe about marriage?

If marriage in the Old Testament was, as I mentioned in the first chapter, primarily an economic issue, marriage for Christians today has become primarily a political issue. To put it simply, the church has politicized marriage.

When marriage is discussed at the national meetings of most Christian denominations today, what matters is who wins and who loses. Both conservative and liberal factions are unashamedly seeking control of their denominations. Church members still debate the issues, and the debates sometimes raise theological points, but it's my impression that no one really listens. The theological content of those debates is disturbingly shallow and rarely persuasive.

The final vote count is always, and in every case, far more important today than what we believe.

Denominations like my own could better serve their own people — and speak more persuasively to the surrounding culture — if they spent more time reflecting on the theology of marriage rather than the politics of marriage. I wish the church would put its considerable energy into lifting up the sacramental dimension of marriage. I wish the church would begin to cherish marriage as the visible sign of God's grace and invite couples to work toward that goal. Perhaps then fewer people would ignore the church's direction and counsel.

On a Personal Note

My personal concern for couples who live together is pastoral as well as theological.

In a recent study, Linda Waite, a researcher at the University of Chicago, found that couples who live together cheat more often on their partners than married couples, are subject to more physical abuse than their married counterparts, and have a greater tendency to divorce when they do get married.

Other long-term studies of announced marriages show that women are worse off financially when one of these relationships ends. It's true that women tend to have a lower standard of living after divorce too, but in recent years state laws have given women a far stronger negotiating position when a pronounced marriage comes to an end. The end of an announced marriage, however, can sometimes leave a woman with no legal rights whatsoever.

This research should be a caution especially to women who believe that living together is a way to test a relationship's viability. More than that, this research should challenge couples who live together to consider more carefully the nature, quality, and depth of their commitment.

In a way, though, the research isn't surprising, is it?

Many of the announced marriages I know about seem to begin casually, without a great deal of deliberation and thoughtfulness. How would those relationships be different if they began with the kind of deliberation and thoughtfulness that I have urged in my chapter on covenant? How would they be different if they set out to be signs of God's grace, as I have described it in this chapter? What would happen if the church began to describe marriage in its sacramental dimensions? Would marriage — a distinctly *Christian* view of marriage — begin to look attractive to these couples?

Conclusion

Not long ago, two dear friends of mine, Mary and Tom, decided to celebrate their twenty-fifth anniversary by inviting friends and family to their church for a vow renewal ceremony. They gave thanks to God and to their families for the grace that had kept them going for twenty-five years, and they said their hope was that their marriage itself might be a gift to all who were present. As a token of that gift, they gave a specially designed ceramic tile to each person present. (I've included the text of this vow renewal ceremony in an appendix.)

Several years ago my wife's parents also decided to celebrate their fiftieth wedding anniversary by renewing their wedding vows. They didn't exchange their vows in front of their entire church family, but they did do it in their church, with their pastor officiating and all of their children and grandchildren looking on. In fact, all of the granddaughters were invited to be bridesmaids — there were quite a few of them — while the grandsons were invited to be ushers. I thought there were more people standing in the "wedding party" that day than seated in the congregation. Which for some reason struck me as just right. After the renewal of vows, there was a dinner and reception in the church parlor, with picture-taking, music, and celebration.

As I think back on that day, what was most important to me was the example of love and faithfulness the rest of the family was invited to witness. I felt as though Susan's parents were inviting their children and grandchildren not just to celebrate a long-term marriage but to see firsthand this visible sign of God's grace in all of our lives.

If sacraments are object lessons in God's grace, then this was an object lesson in the best sense of the phrase.

In the chapters that follow — especially in the chapters on love and power — I plan to say more about what this sacramental understanding of marriage looks like.

Spiritual Compatibility in Marriage

You've got a real problem when two are not, as the Bible says, "equally yoked," together spiritually, traveling down the same street.

W. Frank Harrington, Presbyterian pastor

The Internet has become an indispensable tool for planning wedding ceremonies. A new Web site called theknot.com has advice for just about any aspect of wedding planning — from wedding bands to bridesmaids' gowns to churches.

Reading the site's bulletin board, with all of its posted questions about weddings, is one way to learn a great deal about the modern wedding — perhaps more than you ever wanted to know.

Searching under "church" and "Christian," I found dozens of questions that reveal some of the problems couples are having these days as they attempt to sort through their religious differences. Most couples don't seem to regard these differences as problems — at least not during the planning stages of their weddings — but their questions raise interesting theological issues. And in my experience most of these couples will continue to struggle with these issues throughout their marriages. What seems like a minor wedding-planning obstacle often becomes seriously divisive later in the marriage.

Here's one item on theknot.com bulletin board that I found particularly interesting:

> My fiancé is catholic, but I am not. He wants to get married in the church, however, I haven't decided for sure that I want to become catholic. He's pretty set in his ways, so I don't think he'll look into any other religions. I wanted to know if anyone has taken religious classes in order to convert, and how long the process takes. I disagree with some of the catholic beliefs, so I'm not sure if I want to take this road. Is there any way of getting married in the church even if I decide not to join the church? Any advice would be appreciated. Thanks!

Perceptive readers may see something more serious than religious differences at work in this relationship, but what I as a pastor find most striking about this request for advice is how typical it is. Most of the couples who come to my church looking for a place to get married (and ordinarily that's how the conversation begins) are not of the same mind regarding matters of faith.

Usually they haven't spent much time talking about either their faith differences or — more often the case — their mutual ambivalence toward faith, except perhaps to acknowledge that these feelings exist. Then, as they get caught up in the powerful urge to be married, they project most of these feelings onto the church. And so it's the church that is ordinarily perceived as unreasonable because of its seemingly outdated and odd expectations.

A large number of the couples that I've married over the years have been from different religious backgrounds. I've come to know a certain Catholic priest in a neighboring suburb very well, in fact, because we've co-officiated at so many weddings.

In this respect, things have changed markedly. Only a generation or two ago, people tended to choose marriage partners from their own social, religious, and ethnic groups. When I first started dating (long before I met Susan), my parents strongly disapproved of my desire to date a particular Catholic girl, in spite of the fact that I liked her very much and enjoyed being with her.

51

Very few people today, it seems, experience what I did. People choose marriage partners based on a number of factors, but social, religious, and ethnic factors seem to play a greatly diminished role, and parents rarely seem to raise objections based on these factors, either. As a result, many relationships have built-in obstacles. And while the obstacles don't necessarily doom the relationship, they are significant and should be addressed. Most couples, in my experience, would rather believe that the obstacles don't exist.

My own preference — something I explain to couples during our meetings together — is for couples to choose a particular faith tradition and make it theirs. I believe this choice should be part of the covenant-making process in every marriage. Studies of long-term marriages (those that have lasted twenty years or more) show that most couples who fail to choose, either before or during the early stages of their marriages, generally end up with no religious affiliation. And their children too, according to the same research, reach adulthood claiming no affiliation. Very often, then, not choosing is, in effect, to make a choice.

For some people, agreeing to become affiliated with a specific church or denomination for the sake of a shared religious and spiritual journey can be a difficult matter, one that brings to the surface a number of strong feelings and emotional attachments. On the other hand, as we'll see in the chapter on family, with its discussion of "leaving and cleaving," marriage by its very nature will involve a certain amount of letting go — perhaps even the letting go of a childhood denominational home.

For the sake of a strong and lasting marriage, I believe letting go is often a wise choice to make.

A Tale of Two Faiths

A few years ago a couple came to me to be married, and very quickly I learned that they were from two very different religious backgrounds. His family was nominally Episcopalian, and hers was fervently evangelical. For a few months they went back and forth to both churches — first to the nondenominational evangelical church in town, and then to the Episcopal church. Some Sundays — heroically, I thought — they tried both on the same morning.

In the end, neither church felt just right, and so the two of them began to explore — which led them, one Sunday morning, to our church. He liked what he found immediately, and his parents didn't care much about which denominational choice he made. They were mildly surprised that *he* cared as much as he did.

She liked our worship too, but said she felt uncomfortable just the same. One of our pastors was a woman, and that was a new experience for her. She was also concerned about what her parents would say about her becoming a Presbyterian. But still, she and her fiancé kept coming back. And finally they made the decision to join.

I met her parents for the first time at the rehearsal and noticed how uncomfortable her father seemed. He was obviously having a terrible time — not just with my church but with letting go of his daughter. As the father of two beautiful daughters, I felt immediate compassion for him — and wondered how I would react in the same situation. I tried to be as attentive and reassuring as I could.

That night the father had a conversation with his daughter and future son-in-law. Later that evening he put his thoughts into a letter that they let me read the next day. The letter was beautiful, and certainly it was everything they could have hoped for. The father had finally given his blessing — grudging, but genuine — and his daughter was free to make her choice.

My relationship with this couple has continued over the years, as they've made their way through graduate school and into first jobs, and I've had the pleasure not only of seeing them grow as a couple but also of seeing them continue to grow in faith.

As this example shows, change of this kind can be extremely difficult. But, as this couple knows, it can also be extremely rewarding.

Ordinarily, religious issues surface at the time of wedding planning. The wedding ceremony itself is so full of meaning that even the smallest decisions about what to include and what to leave out can prompt a serious theological conversation.

Many — if not most — of the couples I marry these days — in fact, many of the couples who are members of my church — include a partner who used to be Catholic. Or who still considers himself or herself to be Catholic deep down. Very few people who are raised in a Catholic church and school, I've discovered, ever really stop thinking of themselves as Catholic. So, even if they decided to become Presbyterian, for example, I've found that their theological thinking is still shaped mostly by their early training in the Catholic church.

It would be hard to overemphasize how important this observation is in my ministry today.

Lessons from an Ancient Wedding

Building a marriage on the same spiritual foundation is not a guarantee of marital success. There are no guarantees. But I believe it's the closest thing you can get to a guarantee. And, interestingly enough, the Bible provides us with a wonderful illustration.

"There was a wedding in Cana of Galilee . . ."

Early in John's Gospel (2:1-11) there's a story about a wedding that I believe provides us with a helpful perspective on the issue of spiritual compatibility. At first the reference to a wedding (in 2:1) appears to be an insignificant detail, a small fact inserted into the story to set the stage for what follows. But, as most serious readers of John's Gospel are already aware, no detail in the Gospel is insignificant. The author wants us to know that Jesus' ministry began not just anywhere, but at a *wedding* feast.

In first-century Palestine, wedding feasts were extraordinary events by any standard. For one thing, a wedding feast in that culture was a celebration that lasted for at least seven days. Parents who have planned a wedding reception that lasted only a few hours can begin to appreciate just how big this event was and how much planning was involved.

For another thing, the number of guests — based on the sense of community that existed then — would have been substantial. The entire village, as well as members of the extended family, was invited to the celebration. The wedding in John's Gospel serves as an illustration. Jesus' mother was there, and Jesus himself probably counted as "extended family," but even his friends — the disciples — were included in the invitation.

A few years ago, during a mission trip to Israel, my Palestinian host invited me to come along to a wedding reception to which he had been invited. I hesitated because I hadn't received an invitation. In this country, as you know, showing up at a wedding reception without an invitation is socially unacceptable.

But my Palestinian host didn't understand my reluctance. So he insisted, saying, "You're my guest!" As a Christian he was familiar with this Gospel story and referred to it. I was his friend, he said, and I would naturally be included in this invitation, just as Jesus' friends were included in that other invitation. "It's all arranged," he assured me, but I still felt very uncomfortable, and in the end I decided not to go.

Today I wish I had. I missed out on a wonderful party.

Clearly, our culture has very specific ideas about who is invited to a wedding reception and who is not, but in that culture the community was — and still is — broadly defined.

An important fact, as we'll see.

According to scholars' calculations, Jesus and his disciples had to walk for two solid days from the Jordan River valley just to reach Cana. Walking long distances was a way of life in the first-century world, but even so, we can infer something about the importance of this event from the effort Jesus put into getting there. He dropped whatever he was doing and went. And so did his friends.

Readers aren't told who the bride and groom are, and as far as the story is concerned, their identity isn't important. What is important is that Jesus reveals his own identity in the context of a wedding feast. His ministry begins in the context of celebration. But not just any celebration — a *wedding* celebration. Turning water into wine — as much as 120 gallons of it! — was, in the language of John's Gospel, "a sign," the first of several signs that Jesus performs (2:11). The author rather pointedly doesn't call them miracles, because the signs were seldom important by themselves. What made them worth noting is what they pointed to, and in every case they pointed to Jesus and his emerging identity as God's son. In this story, the changing of water into wine "revealed his glory," leading Jesus' disciples to "believe in him."

More than that, 120 gallons of wine — which is an extraordinary amount of wine and a very fine wedding present — pointed to Jesus as the source of new life. Life with him was definitely not going to be a gray, joyless existence. It was going to be *abundant* life, like going to a wedding feast. The gift of his life was going to be as extravagant as his wedding gift at this feast.

"There was a wedding in Cana of Galilee . . ."

Here, I believe, is one of those places where the Bible says both less and more about marriage than we sometimes think it does.

The wedding feast described in John 2 isn't first of all about marriage. It's only the background against which the real story takes place, and that story, as I've explained, is clearly about Jesus and his identity as the source of new life. Anyone who comes to these verses looking, let's say, for specific hints about how to improve a troubled marriage will be disappointed.

Over the years, I've learned that many well-meaning Christians often read their Bibles in just this way. For that reason I should mention that this story is also not the biblical justification for a return to arranged marriages, which is what the one described in John 2 undoubtedly was. (Romantic love would not become a reason for marriage for many hundreds of years.) Furthermore, there are no guidelines in this story for having much longer wedding receptions and serving extraordinarily large quantities of wine. Those could in fact be excellent ideas, but this story isn't supporting them. As I've explained in previous chapters, that's not how the Bible teaches us about marriage.

So, in a sense, these verses tell us *less* about marriage than we might hope. On the other hand, I've come to see that these verses also tell us *more* about marriage than we might at first think. I've come to see this story, in fact, as providing a very important biblical perspective on marriage.

As I've already noted, the wedding described in these verses was, first and foremost, a community event. I think that's essential for us to see. The bride and groom, whoever they were, were surrounded by family and friends, the people who cared about them more than anyone else in the world. They not only shared the same language and the same customs, they shared the same values and the same faith. And the community reinforced — perhaps even regulated — all of it. In the language of popular culture, we would say that an adequate support system for this marriage was in place.

The unidentified couple may not have been in love with each other as we would understand that feeling today, but they had something deeper and more substantial to assist them in their lives together. They were spiritually compatible.

Culture has changed a great deal since the wedding described in John 2, and I for one have no particular desire to return to the first-century world. Nor do I think that the author is challenging us to make that world our own. The author simply wrote what he knew to be true. This was first-century, small-town life in Galilee.

Still, there's something here we need to pay attention to.

A (Religious) House Divided

"There was a wedding in Cana of Galilee . . ."

Today we have a great deal of romance in our marriages. But we have very little that can be described as community. And nowhere is community more noticeably absent than at a wedding ceremony. As a pastor, I don't often meet couples who've grown up in the same neighborhoods or communities. My wife and I grew up only a couple of miles apart, but our experience is so rare by today's standards that we can almost be considered peculiar because of it.

What's even rarer than a couple from the same community, though, is a couple who brings the same values, convictions, customs, traditions, and cultural expectations to their marriage. A bride and groom today may speak the same language, they may share many of the values of contemporary Western life, they may even share a few interests or hobbies. But increasingly I find that couples today don't share much beyond that.

What concerns me about the marriages I see is that the partners seem to share so few core beliefs. Many couples I marry strike me as having very little in common at a spiritual level. Most couples who marry at my church come from two very different religious traditions, and increasingly one member of the couple comes from a family with no religious tradition at all. Many of the guests at a wedding ceremony today will be completely unfamiliar with church and its worship customs.

All of this, as you can imagine, has had an impact on the wedding ceremony itself. Much of the wedding planning I do with couples today is a conversation about blending two very different sets of religious customs and expectations. What often happens as a consequence is that significant customs get left behind.

Here are just two examples.

Celebrating the sacrament would be an appropriate part of most wedding services, especially from a liturgical perspective. But with so many different traditions represented in the congregation during a wedding ceremony — and given the number of people who often lack a connection to any church — observing the sacrament, I've found, feels awkward and strained rather than celebratory. As a result it's something we don't do much anymore.

We seldom sing at weddings anymore, either, even though a

wedding ceremony is a time to sing if there ever was one. Soloists are frequently employed, of course, but asking a congregation at a wedding to pick up a hymnbook and sing a hymn of praise and thanksgiving can lead to some disastrous consequences, as I've learned from painful experience. Even when the bride and groom have chosen some well-known hymns with familiar tunes, the guests often struggle through a verse or two and then sit down, relieved to be finished. Singing, especially in an unfamiliar place, feels foreign and therefore uncomfortable to most people.

At most ceremonies, the groom's family and friends sit on one side of the church, while the bride's family and friends sit on the other. The aisle at my church is only five feet wide. (I know this because I need to know — brides frequently ask about it.) But I usually see those five feet as an enormous gulf separating two widely divergent groups of people.

Sometimes as I stand there, I look at the bride and groom, whom I have come to know quite well and feel a particular fondness for. Then I look at their gathered families, most of whom I met for the first time at the rehearsal the night before. And what I think is this: "It's going to take a miracle — nothing less than the intervention of God's grace — for this marriage to last."

Without a common faith, without a shared religious tradition, without a shared set of convictions and beliefs, without a community of friends and family, most couples today seem to place the full weight of the survival of their marriage on love alone — in particular, the romantic feelings they have for each other. And as I see it, those feelings simply aren't up to the task, no matter how strong or intense they may seem at the time of the wedding. By itself, romantic love cannot sustain a marriage.

So, here's what I have said to many of the couples who have come to my church to be married: If you don't have a community of friends and family to support you in your marriage, find one. If you have to, create one. Whatever you do, make this a priority, and put it ahead of selecting bath towels and silverware patterns. If you don't have a common faith tradition, choose one. If your wife-to-be is Catholic and strongly connected to her

Catholic faith, consider becoming Catholic yourself. If your husband-to-be is a Missouri Synod Lutheran and can't imagine life outside that tradition, consider becoming Missouri Synod Lutheran yourself. If neither of you feels strongly rooted in a particular denomination, find one that both of you feel a connection to. Be willing to compromise, and be willing to explore the options creatively. That might lead you to a faith tradition that you wouldn't have anticipated. (Many of the couples I marry are surprised that God has led them to a *Presbyterian* church, of all places.)

I have a dear friend in my church who is married to a very fine woman. He grew up Presbyterian, and she grew up Catholic. At the beginning of their relationship, neither was active in a church. Like many young adults I know, they were actively pursuing careers, and faith matters were clearly on the back burner for them.

Several years went by, two children were born, and suddenly — I see this often — faith issues moved to the front burner. They joined my church, they said, because of our excellent Christian education programs. They started to become actively involved in other areas too, but within a year or so my friend's wife began to feel the inner tug of her Catholic roots. She didn't feel at home in a Presbyterian church, and so, after a considerable amount of inner struggle, she began to worship at the local Roman Catholic church. Much to her surprise, the faith of her childhood began to make sense in a way that it never had before. Of course I celebrate the rebirth of her faith.

My friend, however, continues to worship at my church. But now he comes by himself. On Sunday mornings, he goes his way, while his wife and the children go theirs. Occasionally he worships in two different churches on Sundays, his and hers.

For now the arrangement works. But I don't see how it can last. For selfish reasons I don't want him to leave and join his wife at the Catholic church, though I know he probably should. That seems like the compromise that should be made in this situation.

As my friend looks back, he wishes that he and his wife had resolved this issue before they were married. What seemed like such a minor matter in the months leading up to their marriage is now an issue that pulls and tears at the fabric of their relationship. It's a strain they don't need in their marriage.

But my friend isn't the only married person I see worshipping alone on Sunday morning. In my church, many members have husbands or wives who aren't involved in any church and for whom the outward forms of the spiritual life aren't important. Occasionally I'll see these partners on a Christmas Eve or an Easter morning, but in many cases I don't see them even then.

Some of these church members say the situation isn't a problem, that they've learned over the years to live with it. Others, I can see, are hurting because their partners don't want to participate. This is an area of their lives, they realize, that they will never share with their partners. The intimacy that we all crave in a marriage will for them not be possible in this very important part of life.

Conclusion

"There was a wedding in Cana of Galilee . . ."

What existed in Cana of Galilee no longer exists today. Over the years, and especially in the last generation or two, the bonds of both faith and community that are taken for granted in that story have all but disappeared. And so couples today, more than ever before, have to be intentional and deliberate about what used to be assumed.

Marriages are stronger, I think, when they're supported by a common faith, just as they are stronger when they exist within a supportive community of family and friends. When marriage is sacramental, it has two dimensions — one vertical, the other horizontal. The vertical dimension of the sacrament, of course, is God's role in it. But the horizontal dimension is often underestimated in its importance. Sacraments are never personal or private ceremonies. They always, in spirit and by definition, involve the faith community.

Marriage, when it is sacramental, is no exception. To be sacramental, I believe, marriage requires a community. Marriage requires a community to sustain it, just as communities sometimes need marriages in order to be blessed, in order to see and experience God's grace come to life in strong, nurturing partnerships.

You probably won't be surprised to learn that I think a church could provide that supportive community for most couples today. My wife and I certainly aren't the only couple whose families live many miles away. It seems to be the nature of contemporary life to move several times, but seldom to be close to family. My church provides the kind of support to Susan and me in our marriage that we couldn't go without for very long. My church is, in many ways, my extended family. And I know many other couples in my church who would make the same statement.

In the classes I teach for new members, some people candidly acknowledge that they're becoming members of my church for the sake of their children. Typically they express very few needs of their own. They say they want their children to learn the Christian faith — in their words, "to be exposed to it." There are far worse reasons to become members of a church, I suppose, but I would be grateful if — just once — a couple said to me, "We joined your church because we thought it would be good for our marriage."

I believe it would be.

My church, like most churches, is a faith-based community where Jesus is assumed to be a guest at all of our weddings, as he was at that wedding feast in Cana of Galilee. When couples live out their marriages at my church, the hope is that Jesus will be there, sacramentally, in the flesh, revealing himself in the wonderful gift of his presence.

What's Love Got to Do with It?

> *To love perfectly is not simply to see that all else is independent of oneself and so ought to be loved as it is. Perfect love of a living thing is the recognition that it has an inside. To love it is to recognize what it is like to be that object. From the outside it looks gloriously radiant; inside, it is fragile and suffering.*
>
> Diogenes Allen, *Love: Christian Romance, Marriage, Friendship*

I have a friend who is a Presbyterian minister and a clinical psychologist. He's the executive director of a pastoral counseling center in Wheaton, one that provides a number of services to my church — including preparation for marriage.

Charlie Alcorn and his colleagues at the center offer an excellent daylong seminar for couples who are planning to be married, and at one point during the day Charlie makes a presentation to the seminar participants. He begins by telling them he's going to talk about his "three marriages."

That usually gets their attention right away.

He starts off by saying that intimacy in a marriage is extraordinarily difficult, and he knows that better than most people because he's been in three different marriages.

In his first marriage, Charlie explains, he and his wife were passionately and enthusiastically in love. They were rarely out of each other's sight, and their romantic feelings for each other were one of their strengths. Inevitably, though, the romance waned, and the first marriage sadly came to an end. In his second marriage, Charlie says, he spent a lot of time adjusting to his partner, trying to see her and understand her as she really was. He describes this as the marriage that took the most work and provided the least satisfaction. He was glad to see it end. In his third marriage, he says, he at last has found a high level of satisfaction and enjoyment. There's still romance, he reports, though less than in the first marriage. There are still adjustments to be made and even painful times of discovery, though far fewer than in his second marriage. Mainly, he says, there's a healthy acknowledgment of all that makes his partner who she is.

As Charlie tells his story, seminar participants become noticeably uncomfortable. Couples glance at each other, and the looks they exchange seem to say, "Why is *this* guy telling us about successful marriages? He's been married *three* times."

Finally, after holding out as long as he can, Charlie tells his audience that these three marriages were actually with the same fine woman. It's helpful for him and for all of us, he points out, to think in terms of at least three separate marriages or stages of marriage. He believes that nearly all marriages, if they make it successfully through the difficult second stage, will experience the three marriages he describes.

As he gets older, Charlie has started to hint that he may be ready for his fourth marriage, though the exact outlines of that one aren't yet clear to him.[1]

I like Charlie's story not only because he tells it so well but because it's an accurate picture of most long-term marriages I

1. Charlie's insights about the stages of marriage are actually based on a helpful and well-known book by Mel Krantzler, *The Seven Marriages of Your Marriage*. As the title implies, Krantzler has actually identified *seven* different and distinct stages of married life, each with a set of unique challenges.

know — that is, most long-term marriages I know that are characterized by love and commitment.

Most young couples who come to see me about getting married at my church think it's important to inform me that they are in love. Most of the time I don't need to be told. The giggling, hand-holding, and longing looks say it more eloquently than words ever could. Most of the time the couples who sit in my office to plan a wedding are head over heels in love with each other. It's a feeling I remember well. In my own "first marriage," my wife and I were so powerfully attracted to each other that I'm sure our families quickly tired of having us around.

There's a lot to be said for romantic love. I'm a big fan. But how important is romantic love to a marriage? How important is romantic love to a *Christian* marriage?

A Short History of Romantic Love

Some readers might be surprised that I began this book with a chapter on covenant instead of a chapter on love. Love, particularly romantic love, is what shapes the thinking of most people today when it comes to marriage. But from a theological point of view, I've come to realize, a more substantial kind of love plays a dominant role within a marriage.

Love is an important way — perhaps the most important way — that a couple can become a visible sign of God's grace.

If you ask people why they married — and push past the inevitable jokes about toasters and dental insurance — most will tell you that they fell in love. And if they've been married for a long time, they might explain that love means something different — usually something deeper — now than it did when they first met their partners.

Being in love is almost always the reason people give today for getting married. And the loss of love — or falling out of love — is very often the reason people give for wanting to end a marriage. A loveless marriage strikes most of us as a travesty. It's difficult for most of us even to conceive of being married to a person with whom we're not in love. Which is why we're either puzzled or appalled when a financially secure, older man marries a much younger woman — what we call a "trophy wife." Or why we squirm a bit when a widow remarries quickly and incautiously for security. Or why we look askance at southern Asians and Moonies, who are assigned to be married to total strangers.

Romantic love is what we've been raised on. Popular culture is steeped in it. Nearly every movie I've seen in recent years that falls into the category of romantic comedy has a single — if unspoken — message: that romantic love is the single most important reason we marry and stay married to another person. Romantic love is what we hope for, dream of, and expect. If we have it, we can't imagine life without it. And if we don't have it, it's like being deprived of oxygen. We feel as though we'll suffocate without it.

But it wasn't always so.

Romantic love as a reason for marriage is a relatively recent development in human history. It was during the Middle Ages that the idea gradually took hold. Which is not to say that romantic love was unknown in the years before then. We all know the love stories that have come down to us through history. We know from the Bible, for example, that Jacob fell in love with Rachel at the well. We know that Cleopatra and Mark Antony fell in love. So did Tristan and Isolde. And we could go on to name many others.

People in premodern times could and did feel love. They knew love that ranged from companionable affection to passionate desire. Sometimes they even felt it toward their marriage partners (though it was atypical, since many marriages of those eras were arranged). But, according to Princeton philosopher Diogenes Allen, "Prior to the Middle Ages, romantic passion was considered to be a misfortune. In classical times it was friendship that was praised as the highest form of love between human beings." So, declaring romantic love to be a reason for marriage is

66

not only a relatively recent development but also a radical change in thought and feeling.

In a fascinating social history of marriage titled *What Is Marriage For?* E. J. Graff argues that centuries ago people would get married for other, more practical reasons — money, sex, and children, to name the three most important ones. In most societies, across history and across cultures, families would get together to negotiate a marriage contract for their sons and daughters. The families would invariably talk first about money, assuming that after the financial matters were arranged, couples could work out the details of affection, sex, and possibly even love. Sometimes the sons and daughters had veto power over these arrangements. But often they didn't.

Today we are witnessing something altogether new, Graff writes — "the coronation of romantic love as the monarch of marriage." She argues that one of the reasons for the rising divorce rate is our changing sense of what marriage is for. Finding out why societies let people divorce provides "a rearview mirror" answer about what people believe the purpose of marriage to be. "If marriage is for having sex," she writes, "then impotence undoes the marriage. If marriage is for love, then love's loss undoes the marriage."

Apparently love is being lost from a great many marriages today.

And so the question becomes an urgent one. What do Christians believe about love, especially the love within a marriage?

I hope it's obvious that Christians do not embrace the hard-edged notion proposed by some social observers: that marriage is merely a contract in which a woman offers beauty and progeny in exchange for a man's fidelity and security. Not only is that an overly cynical view, but I doubt that it represents — at a conscious level, anyway — what most people today are seeking in a marriage.

On the other hand, we should see that Christian marriage isn't based solely on romantic love, either. I can't think of a single biblical reference or theological argument that would support such a view. Romantic love may — and very often does — lead us to the point where we consider getting married. But romantic love is never by itself a sufficient reason for being married — nor, as we'll see in a later chapter, is the loss of romantic love ever a compelling reason for divorce.

So what do we believe about love?

A Closer Look at 1 Corinthians 13

It probably comes as no surprise to you that most couples, when asked if they would like to choose the Scripture readings for their wedding ceremonies, invariably choose 1 Corinthians 13 — the Apostle Paul's well-known "hymn to love." I lost track long ago of the number of times I've heard this chapter read at weddings.

Occasionally — but in my experience not very often — couples choose other readings, especially when I give them a nudge in a certain direction. But most of the time they select 1 Corinthians 13. And I think I know why.

As I mentioned in the first chapter, the Bible seldom speaks about marriage in the way we sometimes want it to. There are no ten commandments for the married life anywhere in the Bible. If there were, most couples would have a much easier time with this assignment. As it is, many of the couples who are married in my church dutifully search their Bibles in the weeks leading up to their weddings. Most often they make use of the list of suggestions we offer, but even then nothing seems to fit quite the way 1 Corinthians 13 does. The Song of Solomon, one of my personal favorites, is often dismissed as embarrassingly explicit in its sexual imagery, while the other letters Paul wrote appear to place the husband in a position of authority within the marriage. Those obvious alternatives almost never sound like attractive options to the couples who are married in my church.

So, often as a result of choice by default, it's 1 Corinthians 13 that we hear at wedding ceremonies. And as a result many Christians believe these words are the quintessential statement that Scripture makes about love within a marriage. But are they?

1 Corinthians 13 is without a doubt a fine statement about love. It is undeniably beautiful, and there are some scholars who suggest that it was written to be read or sung in worship. While it doesn't say everything that can be said about love, it says a great deal.

Let's take a close look at this chapter. I think there are several important things to notice about it.

First, these words were most likely not written about marriage.

They most certainly can be applied to marriage, but Paul wasn't commenting on marriage when he wrote them. I think it's even fair to say that marriage never crossed his mind as he wrote these words. That's worth noting.

The context of this chapter is a much longer discussion of spiritual gifts, involving chapters 12 to 14. In these chapters, Paul is writing to the Christians in Corinth about the gifts of the Spirit. It appears that they were having quite a conflict over these gifts, especially the gift of speaking in tongues.

What Paul wants the Corinthians to understand is that there are many gifts of the Spirit and that no gift is more important than any other. What's remarkable about the church, he writes, is that each person is given a different gift, which are all then to be used for the common good. At the end of chapter 12, he writes, "And I will show you a still more excellent way."

Given that chapter 13 follows this statement, some readers don't think it really fits here, and there are some scholars who believe that it may have been added later. After all, Paul has just declared that all spiritual gifts are basically equal in importance, so it doesn't make sense for him to say that love is "more excellent."

But there's another way to read these words.

I agree with those scholars who say that 1 Corinthians 12:31 should really be translated along these lines: "So, you want to know about a more excellent way, do you? Then let me tell you about love." Understood in this way, love isn't a spiritual gift — at least it's not in the same category as speaking in tongues. Furthermore, love is "more excellent" only in the sense that everybody needs to have it. Love is what people in the church need to have for each other. Not romantic love, but love of another kind.

Second, Paul never says explicitly what this love is.

He never really gives us a definition of love in these verses. Or, if he does, it's only an indirect definition at best.

Much of the chapter describes what love is not. Love, we read, is not envious, boastful, arrogant, or rude. It doesn't insist on its own way. It's not irritable or resentful. And it doesn't rejoice in wrongdoing.

This language, which is beautiful and suggestive, isn't very helpful in giving us a precise definition of love, but then it's quite likely that Paul wasn't trying to do that. Some scholars suggest — and this makes a good deal of sense to me — that Paul is actually describing here the behavior of Corinthian Christians. They are all the things love is not. They are envious, boastful, arrogant, and rude — to name just a few. And so, far from being a "hymn to love," the chapter is in many ways a strong word of rebuke to Corinthian Christians for their unloving behavior. What they were doing was the very opposite of love.

Third, the Greek word for love that Paul uses is *agape*.

He doesn't use *eros* or *philos,* the two other most frequently used words for love in the Greek language. I think this point is significant too.

Our English word "love" is much less specific than the Greek words for "love" found in the New Testament. When Paul describes love in 1 Corinthians 13, he has a particular kind of love in mind — and it's not romantic love (*eros*) or friendship (*philos*). The love Paul has in mind is much like the love God has for us. Agape love can be described best in terms of divine love.

How would that kind of love help us to understand the love within a marriage?

Fundamental to an understanding of agape love is the loss of concern for self. With agape love a person is able to see another human being as separate and distinct, much as God was able to look at creation in Genesis 1 and say (six different times) that it was "good." God's love was and is perfect love because God sees, recognizes, and respects his creation simply because it is, separate from himself.

This is a crucial point, because often — especially with romantic love — we tend to see our partners merely as extensions of ourselves. Or we notice them only as they orbit around us. We love partly because of what our love for them does for us or how it makes us feel. Freud went so far as to say that all love is rooted finally in infant sexuality. Infants love, he claimed, in order to receive pleasure, and even as we grow older, our love still has this same narcissistic dimension.

Christians believe that human beings are capable of much more. We believe that as a marriage relationship becomes more intimate and as the love in a marriage deepens, the partners are able to see themselves as separate and distinct from each other. When they do, they are moving toward agape love. It's true that this kind of love does not come easily, and that it's not even possible for everyone. Still, Christians believe that this is the kind of love we strive for in a marriage.

But there's more to it than that.

Agape love also has the dimension of compassion. Loving another person fully requires more than recognizing that they are separate from us. When we love with agape love, we recognize what it's like to be that person. In other words, that person is no longer an object to us. Instead, we become aware of that person's inner life, with all of its needs, wants, and hurts.

All of us have a desire to be loved fully, and certainly a large part of that is the desire to be known, to have another person recognize our value, to have our needs taken seriously.

God loves us in just that way.

Even with those who are closest to us, we are seldom able to achieve a love like that which God has for us. Still, that's the goal for love within a marriage. Agape love, God's perfect love.

How Marriage Can Sustain Love

Charlie Shedd, a Presbyterian minister and writer, wrote his *Letters to Karen* more than thirty years ago, but many of his insights about marriage are still helpful and appealing today. One memorable sentence from that book has made its way into popular thought about marriage. Maybe you've heard it before.

"Marriage," Shedd wrote, "is not so much finding the right person as it is being the right person to be married to."

I've always liked that thought, but I've always wondered exactly what it meant to "be the right person." To put it in personal terms, how am I the "right person" for my wife to be married to, and how is she the "right person" for me to be married to?

In an essay in *Christian Century* magazine, L. Gregory Jones, a professor at Duke Divinity School, describes a conversation he had with a student who was thinking about getting married. The student asked an urgent question: "How do you know when you've discovered the best person to marry?"

Jones quickly responded — rightly, I think — that you never really know, that marriage is a commitment made in faith, hope, and love.

The student said he understood all that. He didn't mean "know" in the sense of being certain about someone. He meant "know" in the sense of how you discover, amid all the uncertainties of life, that a particular person is the one with whom you will make a lifelong commitment.

Jones writes that he began by saying the obvious. You need to be sure you're attracted to the person and that you enjoy spending time with that person. There should be a basic compatibility. Most of us would probably add at this point that romantic love and desire would be helpful too.

But, Jones went on, a good marriage should go deeper than all of that. And here's where the conversation became difficult, Jones noted. How do you describe depth in a marriage? Even if you've been in a wonderful, long-term marriage, one characterized by personal and spiritual growth, how do you describe what has happened to you, except maybe in the language of poetry or song? More than that, with what words do you tell someone else not only how to find but also how to become the "right person" to be married to?

At this point Jones says that he blurted out something that surprised both of them: "You should want to marry someone who will challenge the vices you have come to love, and affirm the gifts you are afraid to claim." Both of them sensed immediately that this spontaneous observation was worth further reflection.

In the time since I first read that statement, I've come to believe that it says something important about the marriage relationship, that it provides an enormously helpful description of what love should be within a marriage — agape love.

Most of us are naturally drawn to people who encourage us in our vices as well as our virtues. Their encouragement helps us feel comfortable with who we are. No wonder we seek out their company. Beyond that, if we want to be challenged to let go of our vices, then typically those would be vices we already despise. And if we want encouragement with a particular gift, typically we would seek encouragement for gifts we already manifest.

It's counter-intuitive that any of us would seek out a person to live with who would challenge us to give up vices we love and to affirm gifts we are afraid to claim. And yet, I must admit that this is precisely how personal and spiritual growth occurs. This is how character gets developed. And it's this kind of challenge and affirmation that goes beyond friendship, that seems crucial to establishing a healthy marriage, one that's characterized by depth and commitment.

I know some people who are in marriages in which their partners are constantly challenging vices those people have come to love. And what they say to me is that the challenges don't feel good. The challenges have come to feel like nagging, like a lack of acceptance, like a lack of love.

Obviously, then, there has to be more to this picture.

For marriage to be a relationship where there is depth and

where real growth in character occurs, there has to be both genuine commitment and sufficient time for growth.

First, commitment.

Commitment provides the security or safety in which challenge is possible. Challenge without commitment feels too much like a hit-and-run accident. We find ourselves hurt and bleeding by the side of the road. In order to receive challenges, we need to know that our marriage partners will be there for us as we struggle to meet the challenges — and will celebrate our growth.

In my own marriage, I receive Susan's commitment to it as a wonderful gift. I try not to be presumptuous about it or to take advantage of it, but it does provide a comfortable kind of space in which growth is at least possible. Commitment provides a safe place in which there is no fear of rejection. Commitment is like rich, loamy soil in which love can take root and grow.

Commitment involves an element of trust. We need to know that our partners genuinely want us to grow, that the challenges and affirmations we receive from them grow out of an authentic and sincere concern for us. If we're suspicious of our partners' motives, we won't be able to receive what is being offered to us.

It's important to remember, too, that challenge always needs to be balanced by affirmation. I can't emphasize strongly enough how important this is. I know of too many relationships where one partner can no longer hear the challenge from the other because there is seldom any affirmation there. Then the challenge begins to feel more like criticism rather than an invitation to change and grow.

Second, time.

It takes time for marriage partners to believe that they understand each other well enough to know where each other's vices (and gifts) really are. It's no coincidence that long-term marriages are often the ones where there is the highest level of satisfaction and contentment. Over time, marriage partners can come to know each other very, very well.

My church has many young families. And I am aware both from my reading and from my own experience that the early years of marriage, especially when there are young children, can be quite difficult. Studies almost invariably show that marital satisfaction is at its lowest point during these years. Sometimes the stress shows in the faces of the young families in my church.

One reason a marriage is so fragile in those early years is that there hasn't been enough time for solid bonds to develop. Partners can't see what lies ahead. Often all they see are diapers, bills, and sleepless nights. But eventually children do grow older and become increasingly self-sufficient, leaving their parents more time once again to focus on and enjoy the marriage relationship.

When couples are somehow able to survive these difficult years, they discover, as Susan and I have, that the rewards are enormous. The fragile nature of the relationship gives way to something more, something solid and durable. This is the context in which challenge can be both given and received in the right spirit.

In 1987 the writer Walter Wangerin Jr. published a book called *As for Me and My House: Crafting Your Marriage to Last.* The book is about marriage, but in it he takes an intensely personal look at *his own* marriage. I think the book had such a powerful impact on me because Wangerin is a pastor, and some of the issues in his marriage were issues directly related to life as a pastor. Having said that, though, I believe most people will recognize themselves in the marital struggles he describes.

The largest section in the book is about forgiveness. Wangerin writes that communication is always assumed to be the most essential component in a successful marriage, but that in reality forgiveness is far more important. As he puts it, "Let there be communication, indeed. But let the thing communicated be forgiveness." In a marriage characterized by agape love, he seems to say, both partners need to give and receive forgiveness. I agree.

Wangerin's story, which is at times painful to read because of the unblinking light he shines on his marriage, is about the way he emotionally neglected his wife for several years, until — as he puts it — she became dead inside and no longer felt love for him. Her hurt was deep, and once she identified it and named it, she couldn't let go of it, at least not right away. For a month or more the marriage felt irretrievably broken. The two of them went through the motions of being married, but there was nothing between them. In despair, Wangerin decided that he would have to learn to live without love.

Then one day Wangerin's wife stood in the doorway of his study and said simply, "Will you hug me?" At that moment, he writes, he had finally received from his wife the gift of forgiveness, and all he could think to say was, "Sweet Jesus."

I can say from personal experience that there's nothing quite like receiving the gift of forgiveness within a marriage — unless, of course, it's receiving the gift of forgiveness from God. And actually the two are related.

Grace, we believe, is something God first demonstrated for us, and when we are able to offer it to others, we're simply translating the divine language into our own lives. When we hurt the one we love, and that person offers us the gift of forgiveness, there is no better feeling in all of creation. All we can say is, "Sweet Jesus."

The truth is, we do hurt each other. Marriage is filled with disappointments and hurts and betrayals, both large and small. How could it be otherwise? We enter into marriage with such enormous expectations. And then, because we are flawed and sinful creatures, failure is just about inevitable.

But — sweet Jesus — God has shown us a way through. This is not romantic love. This is divine love, agape love.

What about Romantic Love?

Let me end this chapter with a few words about the place of romantic love in a marriage.

I've argued here that romantic love is inadequate to sustain a marriage. Romantic love may be — and often is — what brings couples together, but romantic love by itself won't support a long-term marriage. I believe that, and my own experience in marriage supports me in my belief. But I don't want to leave the impression that I don't like romantic love — or that I don't see the value of romantic love in a marriage.

I do.

There's more to love within a marriage than romantic love, and certainly there's more to love within a *Christian* marriage than romantic love. But romantic love can play an important role.

Diogenes Allen, whom I mentioned earlier in this chapter, writes that romantic love is a lot like a particular talent you might have. You may discover, he writes, that you have a formidable talent for tennis, but that by itself won't make you a tennis champion. Or you may discover a talent for singing, but that by itself won't make you a concert-quality singer. Talents, like romantic love, need to be developed and practiced. And beyond that, you have to have a strong determination or resolution to make the most of your particular talent. I like this insight.

As Allen suggests, the romantic love we feel for another person can be the starting point for something far bigger, far better. Or it can wither away as quickly and abruptly as it sprouted in our lives. When people talk about the hard work of marriage, I believe they're referring to the effort it takes to get beyond that starting point. When we work at a marriage, it's as though we're developing a talent, nurturing and training it toward its full potential. We're taking a feeling and making it something more.

It's always possible, I suppose, to love another person deeply and fully without the passion and desire of romantic love, but I think that love would require an extraordinary amount of effort.

I know of people in my own community — and church — whose marriages were arranged. They don't talk about it easily, because in our culture it's perceived as something curious or odd, but they have explained to me that they didn't fall in love with their partners, not as we know the experience in this culture. Their parents arranged their marriages in another culture, in another country, and then later they moved to this country. They have all told me that they learned to love their partners over the years. And I believe them. The evidence clearly shows me that they do.

But what a wonderful advantage it is to begin with the powerful attraction that many of us have known in romantic love.

In recent years, theologians seem to have noticed the biblical truth that God's love for us is more than agape love. In biblical history, they say, there is also the inescapable dimension of eros in God's love for us. The God we read about in the Bible sounds a great deal like an ardent lover, a suitor. God pursues us and desires us in a way that defies all logic, that seems reckless.

For some Christians, this may be a new — and even uncomfortable — way of thinking about God. But I think it's a way that fits with the God I read about in the Bible and with the God I have come to know in my own faith.

God is a lover — as passionate and as ardent as there has ever been — and with his love for us he has shown us how to love. Not just with agape love, but with romantic love, the love of passion and desire. Romantic love too can be divine love.

Conclusion

Is love important for marriage? Yes, I think that's obviously true. Particularly when love is defined with its full range of meaning and not simply as the attraction of romantic love.

But is love the most important thing that can be said about marriage? No. Covenant provides the basis or foundation on which the Christian understanding of marriage is built. Then sacrament, as we have seen, serves to explain the quality and perhaps even the goal of a marriage relationship. But love, in spite of the paramount importance that our culture attaches to it, is in reality only one of the ways that God's grace is expressed in human relationships.

As we'll see, there are others.

Sex: Refraining, Reproducing, Refreshing

And what do the words "making love" really mean? In the best sense of the words, making love means that in the sex act the couple makes manifest their love for one another. They make known what was always there, but what is otherwise invisible or ineffable, too deep for words. It's making their love into a palpable experience. It's making a gift of love.

Walter Wangerin Jr., *As for Me and My House:*
Crafting Your Marriage to Last

The Sunday morning that I stood in front of my adult-education class to talk about sex, I was nervous. I admit it. I tried to remember what had possessed me to put this topic on my list in the first place. I can do a pretty good job of sounding knowledgeable about the Bible and church history and a few other topics — but sex? I can't even pretend to be an expert.

My mouth was dry. I looked down at my notes. I tried to smile endearingly. Nothing I did seemed to help. I felt inadequate to the task — and said so.

It didn't help that my wife was sitting in the class that day.

Even now, as I write these words, I'm aware that the topic is large and challenging to discuss. My nervousness is gone, but I realize that so much has been written about sex over the years that one short chapter can't begin to do it justice. On the other hand, something ought to be said, something that helps Christians to think clearly about a difficult and complex topic.

What do we believe — and how did we arrive at those beliefs?

Christians — it must be obvious — are not of one mind about sex and marriage. Nor have Christians ever really been of one mind about these subjects. As with our views about marriage in general, our views about sex have evolved over time. The view of sex that prevailed in the early days of the church is no longer the prevailing view.

What I plan to do in this chapter is what I've done in other chapters — to examine some of the relevant biblical material, to look at church history for some clues about where Christians have been as they've thought about this topic, and finally to offer some general insights.

What Does the Bible Say?

One of my favorite Bible stories is the one found in Genesis 2, where God first introduces Adam to his new partner. Adam's response sounds so real and so touching that I enjoy hearing the words each time they're read. Here's what he says:

> This at last is bone of my bones
>   and flesh of my flesh;
> this one shall be called Woman,
>   for out of Man this one was taken. (v. 23)

Adam is happy and excited, isn't he? There's no word about Eve's response, but Adam's is clear. He takes one look at his partner, and he's aroused. His words aren't terribly profound, but they're full of delight. He likes what he sees. In effect, he says, "Wow."

I think it's significant that sexual longing and desire make their way into the biblical record so close to its beginning. The placement speaks volumes. First, there's the story of creation, of course. That takes up chapter one and most of chapter two. Then, at the end of chapter two, there's the story of the first man and the first woman. (In chapter three the problems begin, but that's another story.)

Sex is important, the biblical narrative seems to say. It's an essential element of the relationship between a man and a woman. It's part of the creation story, so it's part of what God intended for us. And it's a gift, just as the rest of creation is a gift, and for that reason it's something that requires our stewardship, gratitude, care, and wonder.

There's more to the relationship between a man and a woman than sex, of course, much more, but sex is right there — at the very beginning. Sexual longing and desire are obviously woven into the very fabric of creation. As surprising as the thought sometimes is, God designed things to be this way.

Old Testament descriptions of sex are mostly positive. Occasionally, and tragically, human beings distort the good that God intended. There are stories in the Old Testament about awful things human beings do to each other, including rape and incest, and those stories remind us, tragically, that there is really nothing all that new in today's headlines.

When I read the Old Testament over again as an adult, I was shocked by some of the stories I never knew were there. My Sunday school teachers, perhaps wisely, had decided to skip over some of the seamier incidents in the biblical record. But there they are — as part of the story, as a warning, perhaps.

Overall, though, the biblical record is positive regarding sex. As you read, you get the impression that sexual pleasure is supposed to be good and wholesome and life-giving. Nowhere in the Old Testament is the message given that sex is somehow bad or shameful. It can be used in bad or shameful ways, of course, but in and of itself it's clearly something good. Very good.

In the Song of Solomon — or Song of Songs — we're treated to one of the most explicit and moving love stories in ancient literature. The story is really a dialog between a Jewish woman and her lover (presumably Solomon, king of Israel). If you've never read the story before, I urge you to do so.

The lovers in the story describe in intimate detail their feelings for each other and their longings to be together. Here's a relatively tame example:

> How beautiful you are, my love,
>   how very beautiful!
> Your eyes are doves
>   behind your veil.
> Your hair is like a flock of goats,
>   moving down the slopes of Gilead. . . .
> Your lips are like a crimson thread,
>   and your mouth is lovely.
> Your cheeks are like halves of a pomegranate
>   behind your veil. . . .
> Your two breasts are like two fawns,
>   twins of a gazelle,
>   that feed among the lilies. (4:1-5)

As you read the Song of Solomon, you sometimes have to remind yourself, I think, that you're reading the Bible.

Sadly, many Christians over the years have been raised to believe that such powerful sexual attraction is sinful and wrong, something to be afraid of, and certainly not something to be described openly, as it is here. Over the years, probably as a result of this discomfort or prudishness, efforts have been made to interpret the Song of Solomon allegorically — as the story of God's love for Israel or God's love for the church.

It's closer to the truth to say that the story is actually about both — not only the sexual attraction between a man and a woman, but also the way God pursues and desires us. Human beings are created in the image and likeness of God. If sexual desire is a part of human nature, then we shouldn't be surprised to discover that God too is an ardent lover.

Even though this is a love story, it has a refreshing innocence and purity. There's nothing secretive or illicit about the passion described here. What makes the story so compelling is that you sense that this is how God created eros to be. Sometimes love just aches with desire.

Not many couples choose to read the Song of Solomon at their wedding ceremony, and I think that's too bad. Couples sometimes proclaim their love for each other so insistently in the weeks and months leading up to the ceremony that I'm surprised by how solemn and staid they often want to be during the ceremony itself. They will stand primly in front of me as though passion has never crossed their minds.

Who are they kidding? Who is any of us kidding? All of us are born with deep sexual longings and desires. To be human is to want to give and to receive pleasure. I think one of the reasons we enjoy seeing the bride and groom kiss at the end of the wedding ceremony is that the kiss is a confirmation of what we know is true: They desire each other.

I know there's more to marriage than the passion we read about in these verses from the Song of Solomon, but surely it would be appropriate to hear and appreciate this expression of desire in the context of a wedding ceremony.

Unlike the Old Testament, the New Testament has surprisingly little to say on the subject of sex. Jesus seldom addresses the subject, unless asked to. And Paul, most often addressing new Christian converts living in a mostly pagan Roman culture, almost always writes about sexual problems and sexual sin, behaviors that Christians ought to avoid.

In the Sermon on the Mount, Jesus makes the well-known statement about how looking at a woman lustfully is the same as committing adultery with her in one's heart (Matt. 5:28). Although this statement has made its way into popular culture — thanks primarily to Jimmy Carter's reference to it when he was a candidate running for President of the United States — it's not very well understood. When this statement is read in context, it's clear that Jesus wasn't condemning sexual longing and desire — which is how most people today probably hear these words.

As with all of his statements in this section of the Sermon on the Mount, Jesus is calling us to higher standards of respect and honor for each other, beyond what the law requires. When we look lustfully at another person, we may appear to be within the law. But Jesus asks us to remember the spirit or intent of the law.

Looking lustfully at a woman (or a man), he reminds us, isn't the way to show respect and honor for that person. Sometimes our looks and thoughts demean and degrade, reducing other people to objects.

As the Song of Solomon surely makes clear, it's possible to have a strong sexual desire for another person without demeaning and degrading that person in the process. At its best, sexual desire affirms us and makes us feel wanted and desirable. At its worst, sexual desire can leave us feeling used, sometimes horribly so.

Jesus had several conversations and interactions with women that, especially in his culture, would have had sexual overtones, but his attitude and manner are always respectful. He always affirms and honors relationships between men and women. Nowhere does he suggest that those relationships are shameful.

As for Paul's worries about sexual sin, it's quite possible that he had good reason to worry.

In his preaching Paul frequently called new converts to live as though they had been transformed by Christ. He used the language of new life — and even talked about putting to death the old self. But in practice many new converts found it difficult to abandon a way of life that was considered acceptable by the surrounding culture. Hence Paul's frequent nagging on sexual matters. Some of the sexual behavior in the churches he founded was shocking — even by our standards.

Most biblical scholars I know readily concede that Paul would nonetheless have had a high regard for sex as a good gift from God. He was no prude.

But, as we have seen, Paul was convinced that the return of Christ was imminent — that the Second Coming would happen in his own lifetime. For that reason, as I explain in my chapter on singleness, Paul encouraged Christians to avoid the entanglements of relationships altogether. Paul told Christians to remain as he was — single. He urged this not because sex is bad but because, as he saw it, believers shouldn't spend a lot of time thinking about it. All energies, he believed, had to be devoted to getting ready:

> Now concerning virgins, I have no command of the Lord, but I give my opinion as one who by the Lord's mercy is trustworthy. I think that, in view of the impending crisis, it is well for you to remain as you are. Are you bound to a wife? Do not seek to be free. Are you free from a wife? Do not seek a wife. . . . Those who marry will experience distress in this life, and I would spare you that. (1 Cor. 7:25-28)

Not surprisingly, Paul's encouragement to believers to refrain had an impact on subsequent church history — unintended though it might have been.

Christian History and Three Main Views of Sex

Over time, Christians have had three main views of sex. One writer — E. J. Graff, in her book *What Is Marriage For?* — has helpfully summarized them as *refraining, reproducing,* and *refreshing.* To know these three words is to know what the church has thought — and to some extent, where the church continues to think — on the subject of sex.

All three concepts are still very much alive in Christian thinking today.

Refraining

Jesus never married. He devoted his entire life to his ministry. Paul didn't marry, either, and he gave compelling reasons why other Christians shouldn't marry.

With the two most important figures of the New Testament remaining conspicuously single, the stage was set for the early church to have a strong bias not only against marriage but also against sex in the Christian life.

Occasionally the reasons for saying no to sex and marriage were practical. Young women were often attracted to the Christian faith in the early days of the church because of the options it provided. For some, choosing celibacy became a way of escaping arranged marriages. And in general the Christian faith was for many women a vehicle of liberation from controlling parents — and later from controlling husbands.

Much more often, though, abstinence was highly regarded as a spiritual ideal. Giving in to one's sexual impulses was very often taken to be a sign of spiritual weakness. Being able to control one's physical desires — including (but not limited to) sexual desires — was a sign of spiritual maturity.

If men and women couldn't help themselves, they were advised to marry, and if they couldn't keep from having sex, then the purpose of their coupling, they were told, had better be to produce children. St. Augustine believed that sex for any other purpose turned "the bridal chamber into a brothel." Even St. Jerome, an early translator of the Bible, wrote that "an adulterer is he who is too ardent a lover of his wife."

To assist married Christians on their spiritual journeys, early Christian monks and theologians offered help by making sex just about impossible to have. For example, they discouraged couples from having intercourse during times of menstruation, pregnancy, and nursing (which could — and often did — last for as long as two years). They also discouraged sex on holy days — Thursdays (in memory of Jesus' betrayal), Fridays (in memory of his death), Saturdays (in honor of the Virgin Mary), Sundays (of course), and Mondays (in memory of departed souls). Sex was also forbidden during the Lenten, Pentecost, and Christmas seasons, as well as on feast days and fast days. Sex was even discouraged on the wedding night — and for several days afterward — as part of the training for a life of continence.

One medieval Jewish commentator wryly noted that there might be an occasional Tuesday or Wednesday on which a Christian couple could make a baby.

This emphasis on refraining that was so much a part of early Christian thinking never really went away. Views of marriage changed over the centuries, as I've noted in other chapters, but for Christians there has always been a desire to control and put limits on sexual desire.

When evangelical Christians, for example, urge the teaching of abstinence instead of methods of birth control in the public schools, the refraining impulse still seems obvious. I should note, though, that the refraining impulse seems not so much about sex being evil as it is about limiting sex to marriage and encouraging young adults to face the consequences of their sexual behavior.

Still, there is the unmistakable sense in Christian writing today that sexual desire is a mysterious and sometimes frightening force, and that therefore it needs to be controlled, limited, and regulated.

Reproducing

In my research I was amazed to find that for centuries what the church referred to as the "crime against nature" wasn't homosexuality, as it would be for many Christian people today, but rather any sex that attempted to avoid conception — what some writers referred to as "non-begetting sex."

According to one early theologian, if a married couple tried to prevent making babies while making love, the wife was no better than "a harlot and the husband an adulterer with his own wife." If they used contraceptives, this theologian said, "I do not see how we can call it a marriage."

Those are strong words by today's standards. But for centuries this was the church's official position on sex within marriage. Sex was for making babies. Period.

In the nineteenth century, when birth rates began to drop in Western countries, church leaders spoke out against a world of "harlots and adulterers." It wasn't until the middle of the last century that the emphasis on procreation, as the main reason for sex within a marriage, began to fade away.

St. Augustine, whose views on the subject were persuasive for generations of Christian people, outlined three main reasons for getting married: *proles* (procreation), *fides* (fidelity, or avoiding fornication), and *sacramentum* (establishing a permanent bond). He and the theologians who followed him were clear on the order of importance too. Always and in every case, Augustine believed, the main purpose of sex within marriage was procreation.

"I do not see," he wrote, "what other help woman would be to man if the purpose of generating was eliminated." Once again, by our standards, those words are simply astonishing, and yet what's important to recognize is how much our beliefs have changed over the years.

When the Reformers of the sixteenth century came along, they attacked many of the teachings of the Catholic Church, but not Augustine's teachings about marriage. The Reformers were mainly opposed to the idea that celibacy could be the path to a higher spirituality. For them, refraining wasn't the answer; reproducing was. Unlike the Catholics, the Reformers wanted everyone to be married and to enjoy the many benefits of married life.

Luther himself worried about the late age at which so many people were being married. At the time, most Europeans waited until their late twenties, and Luther suspected — perhaps rightly — that this allowed too much time for fornication. Better, he said, for girls to be married at fifteen and boys at eighteen.

Like many theologians before and after him, Luther had a relatively low view of sex. As he saw it, sex was a powerful force that had to be curbed and limited. Marriage, he wrote, was the way "the man and the woman should be taught to keep the passion of lust in check."

Interestingly, by reserving sex for marriage and rejecting the Catholic ideal of abstinence, the Reformers perhaps inadvertently raised the issue of obligation. In other words, if Reformers can be considered strict about prohibiting extramarital sex, they sometimes became equally strict about enforcing sex within marriage. For perhaps the first time in church history, sex was described explicitly by Christian writers as an *obligation* for marriage partners.

In my reading I came across the story of one husband in the Massachusetts colony who was put in the stocks alongside his adulterous wife and her lover. Why? Because, the reasoning went, if *he* had been meeting his marital obligation, *she* wouldn't have strayed. No one knows anymore exactly what was going on inside that particular marriage, but a kind of precedent was set with this legal thinking. People could be punished for failing to live up to their marital duties.

I also came across a Jewish tradition that dates from about the same time. Rabbis actually laid out a timetable for how often husbands would be required to "rejoice their wives." For "men of independent means," the standard was "every day." For laborers, twice a week. For camel drivers, "once every thirty days." And for sailors, "once in six months." Husbands who were derelict in their duty gave their wives grounds for divorce.

Even today some Christian writers raise the issue of obligation. Sometimes they refer to Paul's statements about sex and marriage in 1 Corinthians: "The husband should give to his wife her conjugal rights, and likewise the wife to her husband. For the wife does not have authority over her own body, but the husband does; likewise the husband does not have authority over his own body, but the wife does. Do not deprive one another except perhaps by agreement for a set time" (7:3-5).

While it's true that the Apostle Paul doesn't say exactly how sexual obligations work out in a practical way within a marriage,

I for one can imagine some distortions that could easily result from this teaching and ideas extrapolated from it.

If sex is a gift, and if it's intended for the pleasure of a married couple, which seems to be the biblical point of view, then surrounding it with the language of obligation at the very least raises a red flag. A sense of obligation or duty concerning sex would very quickly rob sex of its purpose within marriage. Sex is something one partner wants to give or offer to the other, not feel obligated to provide.

Maybe it's enough at this point to say simply that a mutually satisfying sex life is a key component of a happy, healthy, *Christian* marriage. And the absence of a mutually satisfying sex life is a reason for couples to get help — or quite possibly, under certain circumstances, to end their marriages.

To return briefly to the issue of reproducing, the Roman Catholic Church remains opposed — officially — to any use of artificial birth control, and from a doctrinal point of view, procreation still seems to be the main function of the sexual relationship within marriage. However, even the Catholic Church has struggled with its stand, and in the 1950s the pope told church members that "husband and wife should experience pleasure and happiness in body and spirit. In seeking and enjoying this pleasure, therefore, couples do nothing wrong." Producing children, in other words, need not be a joyless experience.

A final point needs to be made. If sex is for procreation only, then there are certain logical — though perhaps unintended — implications.

The first implication is how a couple may have sex. Vaginal intercourse would seem to be the only way to produce a baby, and therefore *all* other ways of having sex would have to be regarded as unnatural, as contrary to nature.

First the church, and later the state, seized on this reasoning "from nature" and decided — logically — that only vaginal intercourse was morally acceptable. In the ninth century, based on this reasoning, St. Bernadine of Siena wrote, "It is better for a wife to permit herself to copulate with her own father in a natural way than with her husband against nature," and "It is bad for a man to have intercourse with his own mother, but [it] is much worse for him to have intercourse with his wife against nature."

To twenty-first-century ears, those are astonishing and disturbing words, but they illustrate the horror Christians had — at one time — of all non-begetting sex.

But what if sex is meant to be for more than procreation? Other ways of having sex might be permissible, but which ones? And how do we decide? Laws against "sodomy" — a word frequently used to describe non-begetting sex — are still on the books in several states because people today still haven't fully come to terms with this question: What is sex for?

A second implication of the sex-is-for-procreation-only reasoning concerns *who* may have sex. Two men may not, obviously, but two women may not, either. What about heterosexual couples in which the woman is past menopause? Should *they* be engaging in sexual behavior? Not according to church teaching that existed for centuries.

In the last several decades, this reasoning has been challenged by a new point of view.

Refreshing

During the last half century, there has been a dramatic change — some would say a revolution — in the way Christians think about sex and marriage. Refraining and reproducing have given way to . . . refreshing.

Back in 1549, Archbishop Thomas Cranmer wrote in the Anglican Book of Common Prayer that marriage was for "mutual society, help and comfort, that the one ought to have of the other, both in prosperity and in adversity." In other words, human companionship.

So, after all those centuries, marriage was no longer an arrangement to make legitimate babies or to keep people from fornicating. Being good to your partner and drawing joy from the marriage relationship could actually be a way of pleasing God.

The idea didn't take hold right away — as the discussion in the preceding section shows — but it grew slowly and steadily. And in recent years most thinking about sex and marriage centers on the idea that sex is primarily for marital intimacy. Certainly most books about sex and marriage that I find today — those written from a Christian point of view — enthusiastically embrace sex as an important component of married life. By and large Christians today seem to believe that marriage partners ought to have a sexual relationship because sex is a good and wonderful gift, because physical intimacy and lovemaking deepen and enrich a marriage relationship.

Many Christian writers, it's fair to say, have *enthusiastically* embraced this recent development in thinking about sex and marriage. How-to manuals for giving sexual pleasure within marriage, which might have been unthinkable for a Christian bookstore to carry only a few decades ago, are now relatively common.

Marabel Morgan's book, *The Total Woman,* was one of the first of this genre. It encouraged Christian women in the mid-1970s to embrace their sexuality in some daring new ways — to take bubble baths before their husbands came home from the office, for example, and then to meet them at the door dressed in nothing more than plastic wrap.

At the time, her suggestions for romance in the home created something of a sensation — both in Christian circles and in the mainstream media. A Christian woman encouraging such free and open sexuality was unexpected, to say the least.

More recently, respected Christian leaders Tim and Beverly LaHaye, in a book called *The Act of Marriage,* have provided detailed information to help husbands and wives increase their sexual enjoyment in marriage, including instructions for direct clitoral stimulation. They even suggest that the Song of Solomon recommends this particular practice (8:3).

Marabel Morgan's book was a topic of conversation for months after it was published. No one seemed to bat an eye when the LaHayes published their book.

It's fair to say that most Christians have welcomed this new approach to sex and marriage. An emphasis on refreshing has been a welcome change from the emphases on refraining and reproducing because it seems to acknowledge something central to our created nature.

But the change also raises questions that Christians are just beginning to address.

If sex is primarily for pleasure and intimacy within a marriage relationship, who is to say what's natural and what's not? Sometimes what's pleasurable in sex can also be demeaning or degrading by some standards. Clearly much more remains to be said about how this principle is going to work itself out in the lives of Christian couples.

Sex and the Seventh Commandment

No matter what its ultimate purpose — reproducing or refreshing — sex is and always has been an important part of the marriage relationship. And partly for that reason, adultery has always been recognized as a serious problem in marriage.

Marriages experience stress and strain for many reasons, but adultery must be the most serious jolt a marriage can experience. I've known a few marriages that have survived an extramarital affair and have gone on to be stronger than before, but most often the revelation is so painful, so wrenching, that divorce seems to be the only option.

Adultery comes in many forms. By placing the discussion of adultery in my chapter on sex, I don't mean to imply that a sexual relationship outside of marriage is the only way to be unfaithful. The term "emotional adultery" has been used to describe relationships outside of marriage that may stop short of sexual infidelity, but nevertheless break the promise of exclusiveness within the marriage covenant. Still, adultery is most often associated with sexual unfaithfulness.

As I mention in my chapter on divorce, some of Jesus' sayings in the gospel seem to permit divorce only in cases of adultery — the so-called exemption clause. So destructive is adultery to a marriage, so harmful to its bond of trust, that throughout church history adultery has remained the one unquestioned reason for ending a marriage. In the Mosaic law, in fact, adultery was considered to be such a heinous crime that it was punishable by death (Lev. 20:10).

Imagine that. Adultery was at one time a capital crime.

One couple I know went to see their pastor years ago and told him they were thinking about getting a divorce. He looked at them intently across his large desk, and his first question was, "Who sinned?"

It's a revealing story because for many years it has been assumed that most other issues in a marriage can be resolved. But not adultery. In those rare cases where marriages survive adultery, it's only been after a great deal of work — and forgiveness — that the climate of trust has been restored. A few Christian organizations have even emerged in recent years to support couples as they attempt to mend their relationships after adultery — a testimony to the Christian belief that no sin is beyond God's redemptive power.

From the time of Moses to our own, however, people of faith have been very clear in their understanding of the issue. Don't do it, they have said.

You shall *not* commit adultery.

Why?

The commandment against adultery exists to stake out boundaries for sexual freedom. Sex within marriage, the commandment implies, is such a precious gift that, unless we put boundaries around it, we will end up harming ourselves and others. The temptation is to think that sex outside of marriage is a rather small indiscretion.

It's not. And many people, realizing just how profound an indiscretion it is, take great care not to make it.

I know that there's supposed to be an epidemic of unfaithfulness in our culture today. Studies show that large numbers of men and women pursue sexual relationships outside their marriages. Books and movies, too, seem to describe a world in which people regularly have extramarital sexual relationships. Our own experience — with friends, neighbors, and co-workers — might lead us to think that everyone is doing it. And getting away with it.

A psychologist I know says, "Many times adultery is not a callous act of self-gratification. It's often an ill-conceived way of reaching out for something perceived to be absent from the marriage."

I know all of that.

But I know too many people who have done it and regretted it, who in one act of passion have done irreparable harm not only to their marriages but to the lives of their children, their extended families, and sometimes to their careers. Adultery is almost never a small indiscretion.

I also know too many people who are married — some newly married, but many in long-term marriages — who have demonstrated the courage and good sense to work on their relationships in less destructive and more honest ways. I know too many people who are in their marriages "for better and for worse." They remain faithful to their partners, and they are glad about it. Keeping the commandment has brought them more satisfaction in life, not less. They have discovered, as I have, that sex in a long-term, committed, and exclusive relationship can be good, satisfying, and occasionally wonderful beyond description, perhaps a visible sign of God's grace.

Adultery is always a bad idea. But is it an unforgivable sin?

The short answer is, No.

Jesus, as I mentioned, had relatively little to say on the subject of sex, unless he was asked a direct question about it. In John's Gospel (8:1-11) we read of the time that a woman was brought to him, and the scribes and Pharisees said, "Teacher, this woman was caught in the very act of committing adultery. Now in the law Moses commanded us to stone such women. Now what do you say?"

The way Jesus handled the situation is instructive.

The tension in the air that day was almost palpable. Raw emotion was seething at the surface. The crowd that had gathered was ready to throw stones at the woman; all they needed was the right signal from someone. After all, something had to be done. Punishment was required.

Rather cynically, the leaders saw that this was a terrific moment to test the young rabbi from Galilee and perhaps to make a fool out of him. So they asked him, "What do *you* say?"

Jesus, who knew the law of Moses as well as any of them, could see what they were trying to do. They were intent on killing the woman and discrediting him too. A two-for-one bargain. But he wasn't drawn into the feelings of the moment. Remarkably, he did what most of us could not have done in that situation. He maintained a non-anxious presence. In response he knelt down and drew in the dirt. What he sketched we'll never know.

When the leaders persisted with their questions, he stood up and said to them, "Let anyone among you who is without sin be the first to throw a stone at her." With that he once again bent down to draw in the dirt.

His words had a transforming effect, as they often did. Suddenly the tension was gone. The feelings of rage dissipated. One by one the crowd went away, beginning with the leaders. They would be back again for another round, of course, but for now at least Jesus had gotten the better of them.

When only the woman was left — ever wondered why *she* stayed around? — Jesus stood up again and addressed her with the utmost respect: "Woman, where are they? Has no one condemned you?"

Briefly she confirmed what he could already see for himself. "No one, sir."

So, he said to her, "Neither do I condemn you. Go your way, and from now on do not sin again."

The eleven verses that make up this story are missing from

the oldest manuscripts we have of John's Gospel. Scholars aren't quite sure what to make of that, so they put this story in brackets, as if to say, "We're not sure whether these verses belong with the rest."

I'm not a biblical scholar, but if I had a vote, I'd vote to keep the story in because it seems to fit. It fits with John's Gospel, and it fits with the overall picture of Jesus in the New Testament. He doesn't like sin, and he doesn't hesitate to say what sin is. But he also has a powerful desire to forgive and to teach forgiveness.

It's not the death of this woman that he desires. It's her life that he wants. He wants her to carve a new life out of a broken past.

Even the Apostle Paul, in those harsh-sounding words he hurls at the Corinthian Christians over their careless sexual behavior, is only trying to call them to the new life he knows is possible in Christ. He doesn't tell them off or write them off. He invites them to new life.

Conclusion

The wrestling that Christian thinkers and writers have done over the years on the issue of sex and marriage has often sounded embarrassingly prudish. In some cases Christians have a well-deserved reputation for being scared of sex. Today, in fact, we look back and can see that many early Christians were just plain wrong in the statements they made or in the teachings they presented. Sex is not evil. It's not something that we need to avoid. There may be many good reasons to pursue a life of celibacy, but not because sex is bad and not because celibacy is a surer route to spiritual enlightenment.

Sex, most Christians today agree, is good. More than anything else, it's God's good gift to us. The Bible tells us that's true.

But it's so good, so precious, so awesome, that it needs to be handled with care and wonder, just as the rest of God's creation needs to be handled with care and wonder. Sex is the sort of gift that, without safeguarding, doesn't feel much like a gift anymore. More than most of God's gifts, it's terribly susceptible to abuse. Because our sexual nature is so central to who we are, so much a part of human identity, the potential for hurt and injury is heightened. Sex requires our extraordinary care.

Most of what was written by Christians about sex was written with this in mind.

Power: Subject to One Another

Everywhere the New Testament sings the song of relationships restored, of divided persons reunited with one another, of hostilities overcome and healed. That is the good news of the gospel for every one of our marriages. Woman is restored to her full equality with man. There is in Christ no differentiation in worth or status between male and female.

Elizabeth Achtemeier, *The Committed Marriage*

A few days before Susan and I were married, we bought a brand-new, shiny red car right out of the dealers' showroom. Naturally we were thrilled, and for a couple of hours we took turns driving that new car all over town.

Susan drove the last leg of the trip to her parents' home, and as we swung into her parents' driveway, her father was standing there waiting for us. When he saw the two of us, he didn't look pleased.

I didn't know him very well at the time, but I was pretty sure that the look on his face registered somewhere between concern and horror. After we got out of the car, Susan dashed into the house without a word, leaving me to have an awkward conversation with her father. I didn't know what to expect. He decided to take the opportunity to give me a bit of pre-wedding advice, the only such advice I ever remember getting from him.

"Doug," he said, "you do the driving."

As my father-in-law saw it, the male in the relationship ought to do the driving and anything else associated with the traditional male role in marriage. For him it was as plain as the nose on my face. What concerned him was that I didn't see it. He expected me, not his daughter, to be behind the wheel of our car.

Looking back, I can remember several people who whispered little gems of advice to me in the days leading up to the wedding. But of all the suggestions I received, that's the only one I remember. "Doug, you do the driving."

To be fair to my father-in-law, who was certainly fair to me over the years, he made other observations about marriage along the way that I both treasured and respected. When Susan and I would talk early on in our marriage, somewhat idealistically, about our desire to have a fifty-fifty kind of relationship, he would patiently respond with the observation that, in practice, marriage was rarely ever fifty-fifty.

Drawing on many years of marriage experience, he told us that most days marriage feels like a sixty-forty kind of relationship. And some days, he said, it may even be closer to seventy-thirty or eighty-twenty.

Susan and I were talking about sharing power, of course, having a relationship characterized by full equality and mutuality, but he was trying to tell us — very wisely, as it turned out — that it's tough to achieve balance in any kind of relationship. And so, as he saw it, one partner always has to be prepared to give more than the other is at that moment able to give.

He raised an interesting issue for us, one that most married couples, I now realize, must face early in their relationships.

My observation is that couples wrestle with the issues of power and authority in their relationships more frequently than any other issues. Even issues like money, sex, and in-laws are very often, at their root, about power and authority within the relationship.

The sometimes-unspoken question is, Who's in charge? Or, to put it another way, who has the final word? In a marriage, whose opinion is finally going to carry the most weight?

These are more than just thought-provoking questions, as most people who are married well know. In every marriage there are decisions to be made, sometimes a variety of decisions each day. Sometimes those decisions are about seemingly inconsequential matters, but at other times they have far-reaching consequences. It's often very revealing, as a matter of fact, to explore the dynamics of the decision-making process within a marriage. How a couple works out the issues of power and authority will probably determine to a surprising degree the level of happiness and contentment they have within their marriage.

If a choice has to be made between accepting a job offer in another city or keeping the old job and not moving, who gets to decide? If the choice is between selling the house and moving to Florida for retirement or staying put and tolerating Chicago winters, whose decision is that? At the end of a maternity leave, the choice is between mom going back to work and finding suitable child-care arrangements and mom staying home and becoming a full-time parent. Who gets to make that decision?

Especially in those situations where there is no agreement, who in the marriage has the final word?

If you're a person of faith, you may find yourself wondering what your faith says about these issues. Is there is a uniquely Christian perspective on the issues of power and authority within marriage?

In this chapter we'll explore together the biblical texts that address how women and men are to be in relationship with each other. I believe that the biblical view on this issue is actually quite a compelling one. In fact, it's a perspective that's extraordinarily good news in a culture where there are so many unhealthy patterns of power and abuse in human relationships.

Let's look at what the Bible says.

Relationships in Biblical Times

The world that produced the Bible is vastly different from the world we live in today. Which is not to say that the Bible is therefore irrelevant.

The Bible, as we'll see, has a great deal to say that's relevant to relationships between women and men. But it's important to acknowledge that the worlds in which the Old and New Testaments were written are so different from our own that we need to remind ourselves, even before we read the relevant texts, how much has changed.

Ours is a Western technological society. Ours is a society in which families typically rely on two incomes — in many cases simply to survive. Ours is a society in which single women are frequently the heads of their households. Ours is a society in which there is a growing acknowledgment of gender equality. Ours is a society in which both mothers and fathers are expected to care for and raise their children. Ours is a society in which arranged marriages are exceedingly rare.

Contrast our society, then, with the world that produced the Old Testament — Near Eastern, nomadic, patriarchal, pre-industrial, to name but a few characteristics. Falling in love as a reason for getting married was virtually unknown in those times. (The reference in Genesis 24:67 to Isaac's love for Rebecca certainly sounds genuine, but most of us would stop short of saying that their marriage is a model for us. As the years passed, in fact, Isaac and Rebecca's marriage was scarred by betrayal and trickery.) There is no Hebrew equivalent for our modern English word "family." The closest term is perhaps *bet ab*, which literally means "father's house." The term describes the male-dominated, multi-generational household that was the basic family unit in ancient Israel. Accepted customs included polygamy and the requirement that a male relative marry any childless widow in the family.

It's fruitless to look to the Old Testament to find any role models for modern marriage. They're just not there.

What the Old Testament teaches us, though, is that God is at work in all human relationships, including marriage and family relationships. We learn, too, that promises are made to be kept and that, when they're broken, suffering and conflict will occur. We can also learn from the Old Testament the value of the extended family. There is security and a profound, almost fearless sense of self-worth that comes from being born into a family that has an ongoing relationship with God. Finally, the Old Testament may even speak a word of judgment about the idolization of the family that occurs in our culture. We sometimes think of our marriages and families as having ultimate importance, but the Old Testament emphatically reminds us that they, like everything else in creation, exist to glorify God and to serve God's purposes of grace and redemption.

Relationships from Genesis to Jesus

Elizabeth Achtemeier, a Presbyterian teacher and theologian, has taken a careful look at the first few chapters of Genesis, hoping to discover there what the Bible teaches us about power and authority within marriage. Her insights can be instructive for us. God's intent for women and men, she writes, is that they be free and equal: "There is no hint whatever of any superior or inferior station."

How an author in the ancient Near Eastern world could have laid hold of such a view, she says, "seems beyond rational explanation." Remarkably enough, God intended no subordination, but full equality between women and men.

What God intended, however, changed dramatically with the Fall. In Genesis 3, the idyllic situation that God created for women and men came to an end — and with that change came conflict and chaos. And so, rather ominously, God said to the woman, "[the man] shall rule over you" (Gen. 3:16).

But what's important to note is that this is a *corruption* of what God intended; it's what happened when human beings denied their relationship with God. In much of the rest of the Old Testament, according to Achtemeier, we read about "the brokenness of life apart from God."

Achtemeier says that over time what happened in the Fall became the norm. What she calls the "transcendental vision of equality" was lost, the law was elevated to supreme importance, and women became increasingly marginalized and segregated within Jewish society.

It was into this world that Jesus emerged with words and actions that seemed both alien and intrusive.

In John's Gospel we find a story about a lengthy conversation Jesus had with a Samaritan woman at a well (4:7-30), a conversation *he* initiated. When his disciples saw what he was doing, they were "astonished that he was speaking with a woman" and asked him point-blank, "Why are you speaking with her?" No men in first-century culture engaged women in thoughtful, public conversation.

But Jesus did.

Jesus' closest friends, according to the Gospels, included women named Mary, Martha, and Mary Magdalene. His ministry of teaching and healing always seemed to include both women and men. He even used women as the main characters in his parables (e.g., Luke 15:8-9). And always they are portrayed in respectful and even admiring ways. Sometimes they are held up as models of faithfulness (Mark 12:41-44) — for the disciples!

Finally, women were the first witnesses to Jesus' resurrection — as well as the first evangelists. Ironically, the first witnesses to his birth — the shepherds — and the first witnesses to his resurrection — the women — were not regarded by first-century authorities as trustworthy witnesses. Their claims would have been considered to be unreliable testimony in a courtroom. And yet, the Gospel writers seem to delight in emphasizing these reversals of expectation.

Women continued to play important roles in the early church. We are told in the book of Acts that both women and men were imprisoned by Saul for their faith (Acts 8:3; 9:2).

Women were teachers too. When Apollos was proclaiming a faulty or incomplete version of the gospel, it was Aquila *and* Priscilla (Acts 18:26) who "took him aside and explained the Way of God to him more accurately." In Paul's letter to Timothy, Paul holds up Timothy's mother, Eunice, and his grandmother, Lois, as examples of faith (2 Tim. 1:5). Paul also mentions, in a matter-of-fact way, that women were serving as deacons in the church (Rom. 16:1). And in Hebrews 11, that well-known chapter about heroes of the faith, two Old Testament women — Sarah and Rahab — are mentioned right along with the men. They are included in the "cloud of witnesses."

In the life, death, and resurrection of Jesus, something important had been restored — namely, God's intent for women and men.

The Apostle Paul, a male who was undoubtedly shaped and influenced by first-century culture, nevertheless recognized this restoration, even if he didn't always see its full implications. Something happened in the death and resurrection of Christ, he realized, that changed the entire course of history. In Christ what had been broken in the Fall was restored — and decisively so. And so he was able to write, "As many of you as were baptized into Christ have clothed yourselves with Christ. There is no longer Jew or Greek, there is no longer slave or free, there is no longer male and female; for all of you are one in Christ Jesus" (Gal. 3:27-28).

For Paul this is the hope of the gospel. In Christ, broken relationships are restored, old hostilities come to an end, the walls that once divided us come tumbling down. And this hope, we believe, extends to all human relationships, including marriages. In Christ we believe that women and men are able to live together as God first intended — with full equality and mutuality. To insist on old patterns of hierarchy and subordination would, in a sense, be to deny the power of the resurrection. Obviously the gospel isn't good news if nothing in our world has changed.

But, as Paul knew, something did change.

Challenging Passages in the New Testament

At this point it will be helpful to examine several New Testament passages that have been problematic in terms of interpretation. This will help us clarify what Scripture is saying about relationships within marriage.

Ephesians 5:21-33

Let's start by looking at a difficult passage in Ephesians 5. In verses 22-23 Paul writes, "Wives, be subject to your husbands as you are to the Lord. For the husband is the head of the wife just as Christ is the head of the church, the body of which he is the Savior." All of that is clear and undeniable.

For centuries Paul's words have been taken to mean that — in spite of the resurrection, in spite of Paul's clear statement that in Christ "there is no male and female" — husbands have authority over their wives. Husbands should love their wives, but they must also remember that they are "the head" of the marriage. For many Christians over the years, these words have seemed to be calling women and men to traditional roles within marriage.

As my father-in-law put it, "Doug, you do the driving."

Many Christians, in fact, have taken these words and extended them into the basic biblical principle that God has ordained female subordination to male authority. Some Christians continue to believe, based on their reading of these verses, that the ordained ministry should be reserved for men only. Men are called, they say, to exercise spiritual leadership in the home *and* in the church.

But is that really what these verses say?

It's important for us to see that not all Christians accept this interpretation. Even a substantial number of theologically conservative Christians don't accept this interpretation.

The crucial verse that some interpreters seem to have overlooked is the one that occurs just before the one that begins,

"Wives, be subject to your husbands. . . ." In 5:21 Paul begins the entire section — which includes instructions for husbands and wives, children, and finally slaves and masters — with these important words: "Be subject to one another out of reverence for Christ." Another translation puts it this way: "Out of respect for Christ, be courteously reverent to one another." The Living Bible puts it in an even more striking way: "Honor Christ by submitting to one another."

Any way you translate these words, they are remarkable.

More important, they appear to be Paul's starting point, his thesis, for what follows. In other words, the several statements that follow should be read as providing a further explanation or amplification of this opening statement. Which is that our marriages — and all relationships in the Christian life — are to be characterized by a radical kind of mutuality, what has come to be known as "mutual submission."

Remember, the first-century culture that shaped and influenced Paul would have found this statement alien and even alarming. To some people in the twenty-first century, this statement is still alarming. But clearly Paul offers something here that is a uniquely Christian point of view. In Christ, he is saying, something new and profoundly different is possible within marriage.

When Paul's statement concerning mutual submission is emphasized, several other questions begin to emerge. For example, if the biblical principle here really is mutual submission, then what does it mean when Paul says that "the husband is the head of the wife"?

Scholars have seen in these verses, as well as in other places in the epistles, references to what they call "the household code literature." What seems clear is that Paul didn't question the social and economic organization of the Greco-Roman world. Nor did he question the prevailing hierarchical worldview. The husband was still expected to be the head of the family, and slaves (mentioned a few verses later) were still expected to obey their masters.

One scholar suggests that the way to resolve this apparent contradiction is to recognize that Paul was trying to preserve male "headship" in terms of title or function only, not in terms of status or superiority. Since this was the only model Paul had to work with, it makes sense that he attempted to transform it, maintaining the language but radically altering the meaning.

Other scholars have argued that while Paul certainly recognized the transforming power of the resurrection, he didn't always anticipate the dramatic implications of what that meant. And for that reason he could say in one breath that men and women should submit to each other in marriage, while in the next breath he could say that a man was still somehow to be the head of the wife.

We may never know exactly why he wrote as he did, but we do know this much: As far as Paul was concerned, the death and resurrection of Christ changed everything about life as we know it. He makes that point clear throughout his letters. God in Christ was reconciling the world to himself — and that reconciling work extends to all areas of life, including marriage, the key relationship between women and men.

In my work with Christian people over the years, I've noticed that the resurrection doesn't figure very prominently in their thinking — and certainly not as prominently as it figured in Paul's thinking. Ask most people today what the resurrection means to them, and they'll probably respond by talking about life after death — which is true enough for Christian belief. The resurrection of Christ, we believe, makes possible our own resurrection to eternal life. But beyond that, most Christians I've known have been largely silent. They don't seem to have learned that the resurrection has implications for the rest of their lives as well.

Here are a couple of questions you may want to ask yourself as you come to terms with these words: First, how does the fact of the resurrection change the way you live? And second, and more to the point, how does it change the way you think about marriage? In other words, what's the connection between the resurrection of Christ and your marriage? Paul certainly saw the connection.

These are important questions for all Christians to ask themselves.

Let's continue our look at the relevant biblical texts by looking briefly at three more places where Paul wrote about the roles of women and men.

1 Corinthians 14:26-40

In 1 Corinthians 14:26-40, Paul offers guidance for behavior in worship, including this instruction:

> As in all the churches of the saints, women should be silent in the churches. For they are not permitted to speak, but should be subordinate, as the law also says. If there is anything they desire to know, let them ask their husbands at home. For it is shameful for a woman to speak in church. (vv. 33b-35)

Because of words like these, Paul has developed a perhaps-undeserved reputation as someone who is not a friend of women. The guidance Paul offers here is admittedly not about marriage, but the command to "be silent" certainly appears to have implications for our understanding of power and authority within marriage. A superficial reading of these words certainly seems to suggest that a man's voice or opinion in the church outweighs that of a woman.

One scholar has pointed out that this is a rather strange regulation from someone who repeatedly fights slavery to the law and who repeatedly argues that we are no longer under the law but under grace. This same scholar points out that Paul contradicts himself earlier in the book (1 Cor. 11:4-16) when he allows women to prophesy in worship (providing they follow the first-century custom of covering their heads).

I think the contradiction actually offers a way for us to understand what's really happening here. The situation in the Corinthian church was an interesting one. Not only were they a contentious group of people, but their behavior in a variety of areas left a great deal to be desired. Paul refers to these behaviors throughout the first letter, and they become for him "teaching moments" about a variety of issues.

Worship in the Corinthian church appears to have been a particular problem — in ways it would be hard for us to visualize today. Drunkenness during the Lord's Supper, for example, is just one issue that Paul finds it necessary to address in this letter. Another problem in worship seems to have occurred when a particular group of women, thoroughly enjoying their new freedom in Christ, spoke out whenever they felt like it. To these women, Paul writes in effect, "Be quiet! Let's remember who we are and what we're doing."

His words are harsh and possibly even shaming, but we can infer from them that the problem was a serious one. And Paul wasn't one to mince words. His concern, it's vital for us to notice, was entirely practical. He was looking out for order and decorum in the worship of one particular church. He was not, as some have maintained, laying out a principle for the future role of women in the church.

1 Timothy 2:9-15; Titus 2:3-5

The last two texts that we'll consider as part of this discussion are found in 1 Timothy and Titus:

> Women should dress themselves modestly and decently in suitable clothing, not with their hair braided, or with gold, pearls, or expensive clothes, but with good works, as is proper for women who profess reverence for God. Let a woman learn in silence with full submission. I permit no woman to teach or to have authority over a man; she is to keep silent. For Adam

was formed first, then Eve; and Adam was not deceived, but the woman was deceived and became a transgressor. Yet she will be saved through childbearing, provided they continue in faith and love and holiness, with modesty. (1 Tim. 2:9-15)

Tell the older women to be reverent in behavior, not to be slanderers or slaves to drink; they are to teach what is good, so that they may encourage the young women to love their husbands, to love their children, to be self-controlled, chaste, good managers of the household, kind, being submissive to their husbands, so that the word of God may not be discredited. (Titus 2:3-5)

Most scholars believe that the words addressed to Timothy were once again about specific problems — this time in certain unnamed congregations. What seems to have happened is that the gospel provided a radical new freedom to women, and some women took that freedom to problematic extremes, so Paul is telling Timothy here to instruct them in more modest and traditional behavior. Furthermore, some of the women were acting like "gossips and busybodies, saying what they should not say" (1 Tim. 5:13). As a countermeasure, Paul forbids women to teach in the church and instructs them to pursue more traditional roles.

Paul's words to Titus are very similar, although the women in this case aren't "gossips and busybodies." They're slanderers and drunks! It's important to see here that traditional roles for women are encouraged not because they're expected of all women, but so that "the word of God may not be discredited." Paul was understandably eager not to have his missionary work undermined by the behavior of a few converts.

To sum up, those who wrote these New Testament letters — chiefly Paul, though there were others — understood the transforming and life-changing nature of the resurrection. Because of Christ, they clearly saw, life was going to be radically different.

On the other hand, these same writers didn't immediately abandon all of their old notions about the role of women. When confronted with specific problems in local congregations, they rather quickly reverted to the traditional view of a woman's place — sometimes with the best of intentions, as we saw in the letter to Titus.

Most interpreters of the Bible today would say that these practical instructions to local churches don't change or soften the fact of what Christ has accomplished for us. And more than that, these practical instructions shouldn't be raised to the level of biblical principle. We need to treat these words as we do similar words regarding slavery. (See Colossians 3:22; Ephesians 6:5-8; 1 Timothy 6:1-2; Titus 2:9; and 1 Peter 2:18-25.) No one regards any of those instructions about the relationship between master and slave as having authority for us today.

Christians continue to discover the broad-ranging implications of the gospel. We make new discoveries every day.

What Is Mutuality?

A complete description of the way that full equality and mutuality work out within a marriage, practically speaking, is an area that's beyond the scope of this book. Over the years the best-seller lists have included numerous books that try, with varying degrees of success, to work all of this out. Christian bookstores, I've noticed, sometimes offer dozens of titles on this particular subject.

What I can offer is my own brief take on the way that mutuality works. All of us — women and men — have particular gifts. We bring these gifts to our relationships with each other. When our partners clearly have certain gifts for doing certain things, we acknowledge them. In effect, we submit to our partners, not simply in one area but in many areas of our life together. And in so doing, we honor our partners as well as the God who provided those gifts.

112

In my own marriage, I'm grateful to have a partner who complements me so well. In several areas where I am severely challenged, Susan has been blessed with an abundance of just the right gifts. Not only my faith but my common sense tells me to submit to them. And I do — most of the time. My hope is that I bring a few gifts to our marriage as well, so that in the end we're stronger together than we would be apart.

This is not to say that traditional roles play no part in our marriage — or in most marriages today. Gospel or no gospel, cultural expectations for the relationships between women and men play a powerful role. It's important for us to acknowledge how powerful those expectations are.

In case you wondered, I took the advice of Susan's father and do most of the driving when Susan and I are in the car together. The truth is, she's a much better driver than I am, especially under certain conditions. I probably should submit to her in this area, as I do in several others. But I don't. I can't really account for that, except to admit that both of us have given in to the culture around us. I do the driving, but I'm well aware that Susan can drive too.

To me, if not to all Christians, recognizing the importance of mutuality within marriage just seems like common sense. Happily, though, some recent clinical studies strongly endorse it as well.

John Gottman is a leading marriage researcher, and in one of his studies he found that husbands who share power and control within their marriages are less likely to divorce than men who resist their wives' influence. When husbands aren't willing to share power — in theological terms, to practice mutual submission — 81 percent of those marriages end in divorce. It's important to note that there were other factors that contributed to those divorces, and in studies of this kind it's virtually impossible to isolate any one factor. Still, Gottman's research demonstrated that this resistance to mutuality was a critical or decisive factor in the breakdown of these marriages.

Conclusion

Paul Tournier was a Swiss physician whose medical practice led him to reflect deeply on marriage and family matters. He was a Christian and a prolific writer too. Several of his books have had a profound effect on the way I think, and I know he's influenced others in a similar way.

Tournier died a few years ago, but before his death he agreed to be interviewed for a magazine article. The reporter at one point asked him if could name the secret to a successful relationship. According to the story, Tournier didn't hesitate for a second. I don't remember his exact words anymore, but this is essentially what he said: "The key to a successful relationship is each partner helping the other to achieve his or her full stature."

I've liked that comment since the first time I read it. And I use the story often in my wedding sermons, especially when couples ask me to read from Ephesians 5. To me, Tournier's words describe the kind of mutuality that lies at the heart of a Christian understanding of marriage.

"Be subject to one another out of reverence for Christ." How have you applied those words to your own relationship? Do you practice mutual submission in your own life and marriage?

Leaving and Cleaving:
All about Family

From the beginning, at least as the scriptures report it, the task has been the same: one must leave home in order to get married. While the ways of leaving home and the images of marriage have changed through the centuries, what is necessary to become married has not changed: leaving home.

Herbert Anderson and Robert Cotton Fite,
Becoming Married

The two-step process of "leaving and cleaving" has a long history. As a matter of fact, it's the very first lesson the Bible teaches people of faith about marriage. In Genesis 2, soon after the first woman is introduced to the first man, we find these words: "Therefore a man leaves his father and his mother and clings to his wife, and they become one flesh" (v. 24).

The King James Version of the Bible uses the word "cleaves" instead of "clings," a translation I happen to prefer, maybe because the words "leaves" and "cleaves" have a strong rhyming quality that "leaves" and "clings" do not. "Cleaves," however, isn't a word that's used much anymore except in its other, more familiar meaning — to sever or to part. But "clings" has the unfortunate connotation — in our culture, at least — of suggesting de-

115

pendency. A parasite, for example, clings to its host, and sometimes there are people in our lives — including marriage partners, I suppose — who cling to us in unhealthy ways.

Unhealthy clinging is not the meaning the biblical writer has in mind when describing the relationship of the first man and the first woman, and that's why I suggest we re-acquaint ourselves with the older word.

"One flesh" can be understood in a number of ways. At one level, of course, it refers to a sexual joining. When a man and a woman become "one flesh," there is an implied sexual bond. Others have understood the term to refer to offspring. In other words, a union is not complete until it results in the "one flesh" of a child. But the biblical expression is actually far richer than either of those interpretations. "One flesh" refers not only to the physical but also to the emotional and spiritual union of two people who commit themselves to a lifelong partnership — in other words, who do the work of leaving and cleaving. As I've argued earlier, "one flesh" is the sacramental ideal to which all married couples aspire.

"One flesh" implies more than a covenant relationship; it implies a relationship that is a mystical union.

More than one scholar has noted that Genesis 2:24 contains an odd reference. It says that *a man* leaves his father and his mother. In a patriarchal culture, it was typically *the woman* who would have left her parents and family to become part of the husband's extended family. In many parts of the world today, that's still the case. And so the wording of this particular verse is problematic.

It's possible, as Old Testament scholar Gerhard von Rad suggested many years ago, that these words contain a remnant of a very old and now extinct matriarchal culture — and hence the man, not the woman, was expected to leave his father and his mother.

Whatever the explanation, I think it's important for Christians to see that leaving and cleaving is one way of describing the emotional work of marriage. It's work that *both* partners must do

116

for the sake of a happy and satisfying relationship. Leaving and cleaving lead to the mystical union described in the expression "one flesh."

The insight contained in Genesis 2:24 is in many ways an extraordinary one, and I wonder sometimes if Christian people realize how extraordinary it really is. It's a bit of wisdom that has stood the test of several thousand years, as a matter of fact — and it's as true today as it was when it was first written. If you want some practical advice that's thoroughly biblical, you can't do much better than this.

When two people are married, two separate actions are required — first leaving and then cleaving.

Let's look at each in turn.

Leaving: Harder Than It Sounds

People who are planning to be married must leave home in an emotional or psychological sense. Psychologists describe this clinically as "differentiation from the family of origin." In popular culture most people would call it "growing up," "making your own way in the world," and "becoming your own person."

Whatever it's called, it's a lot harder than it sounds. It also takes more time than most people realize. But it's absolutely essential, because without it the second step — cleaving — cannot take place.

What sometimes happens is that people use marriage as a way of accomplishing the first step. They get married as a way prying loose from the bonds of their family of origin.

In some cases the strategy works, but often it doesn't. Over the years I've known married people who work on both steps simultaneously. As they let go of their families of origin, they are able to build stronger emotional ties with their marriage partners. It's not easy to accomplish both steps at once, but it can be done. I know of many more married people, however, who try to skip the first step altogether. They move directly to cleaving, or try to, without ever having done the hard work of leaving.

As even the ancients realized, there can be no cleaving without a proper leaving.

Psychologists say that even when the process of leaving goes relatively well, the first few years of marriage will contain a few of the residual struggles for independence and autonomy.

In my own experience, the decisions that my wife and I had to make about where to spend holidays and how to combine holiday traditions were more about leaving home than they were about the holidays themselves. I couldn't see it at the time, but it seems obvious to me now. Only when Susan and I had both emotionally left our families of origin were we able to make good, clear decisions about what was best for the two of us. When we had completed the hard work of leaving, we were freed to do what turned out to be the even harder work of cleaving.

The truth is, the process of leaving is far more varied and complicated than it might at first seem.

Our culture may be the first one in centuries, quite possibly the first one ever, where young adults have been encouraged to leave home well before entering into a marriage. Centuries ago, getting married — or having a marriage partner chosen by parents — was a first step toward adulthood, something like getting a driver's license would be today.

In our culture it's not at all unusual for young adults to go away to college, establish careers, and then live for long periods of time as singles. Sometimes this moving away is connected to an emotional separation from the family of origin, which in general is a healthy and necessary step toward adulthood. Often, though, the ties to the family of origin remain intact despite the physical distance.

A young man in my church tells me that he brings his laundry "home" on weekends for his mom to do. It's just a guess, but I suspect he still has some work to do to achieve what psychologists call "differentiation." Simply moving out of one's parents' home doesn't accomplish what the Bible means by "leaving mother and father," but for some at least it's a start.

Most often the decision to be married sets the process of leaving into motion. How the announcement is handled, the parents' response to the announcement, and even the decision to live together before the wedding can all be decisive factors in the leaving process.

When Susan and I decided to get married, we kept the decision a secret for a few weeks until we could tell both of our families. I was going to school in New Jersey at the time, and she was living in Michigan. We wanted to go to our parents together with our news. When we arrived at her parents' home, Susan simply opened the door and announced to everyone who could hear her, "We got engaged!" I assume that having three older sisters who were already married softened the blow of this rather abrupt announcement. We had been in a committed relationship for well over a year by that time, too, so the words themselves probably weren't all that surprising.

Still, in hindsight, I wish we had done it differently. I wish, for example, that I had gone to Susan's parents and discussed my plans to propose with them. If they had had questions or reservations about our marriage, I would at least have given them an opportunity to express them. As it turned out, Susan's parents handled our announcement rather well, but even so I wish I had had the maturity to ask for their blessing before I popped the question.

In most cases, the appropriate handling of engagement details goes a long toward making a healthy leaving possible. I remember reading somewhere that in most cases eloping is a "sneaky leaving." Couples who elope might say when asked that they took pre-emptive action to avoid unpleasant family issues, but psychologists have found that eloping often does little more than avoid the hard emotional work of leaving. Eloping either postpones or subverts the process.

When parents have objections to the person their son or daughter plans to marry, that too adds a wrinkle to the leaving process. I've known situations where parental opposition to the choice of a marriage partner was so strong that an emotional cut-off was the result. In those situations, it's not unusual in my experience for one or both of the parents to refuse to be a part of the wedding ceremony.

Parental objections to the proposed marriage partner don't necessarily doom a marriage. In fact, for some relationships they strengthen the marriage bond by creating a common enemy. I sometimes wonder, though, what happens when the enemy dies, goes away, or somehow ceases to be an enemy. Once again a proper leaving in those cases is simply postponed.

The decision to live together can have as much to do with leaving as it does with cleaving. In an earlier chapter I argued that living together may actually be a form of announced marriage. Couples who live together, whether or not they want the church's blessing, often have what would have been known centuries ago as an announced marriage. I still think that's true, and so here I simply want to point out that living together can also be — and occasionally is — part of the leaving process.

Sometimes, though certainly not in every case, the decision by young adults to move in together turns out to be a clumsy and not particularly well-advised way of trying to leave home. Sometimes couples who move in together anticipate the objections of their parents over their planned living arrangements and keep them a secret until they've set up housekeeping. I would say that these situations fall into the same category as eloping and could be considered "sneaky leaving."

In a book called *Becoming Married,* which I cite at the beginning of this chapter, Herbert Anderson and Robert Cotton Fite focus more on the leaving end of the Genesis 2:24 equation than on the cleaving. They're both Christian pastors, one a Lutheran and the other an Episcopalian, but they write primarily from a psychological or therapeutic perspective. Here's how they describe leaving: "One must be emotionally separated from one's parents in order to become emotionally committed to another person in marriage. Effective differentiation from one's originating family makes commitment to forming a new family possible."

In my chapter on covenant, I encourage couples entering a marriage to consider writing a covenant for themselves. I believe it's important for couples to come to some explicit agreements on the basic issues involved in living together with another person, even if those agreements are changed or modified over time. Anderson and Fite move in another direction entirely, and I believe that direction is worth our consideration. They might agree that writing a covenant is an act of cleaving, but it's one that ignores a necessary and prior act — namely, the act of leaving.

And so they encourage couples to be as thoughtful and deliberate about their leaving as I have encouraged them to be about their cleaving. Anderson and Fite suggest that couples who are moving toward marriage make a point of exploring their families of origin and carefully assessing where they came from.

The co-authors provide elaborate instructions in their book for constructing genograms, which look like family trees with bits of crucial data written next to the names of parents, sisters and brothers, aunts and uncles, cousins, and more. The authors describe genograms as "tools for story telling." What they want couples to do, they say, is to look backward so that they can look forward and blend their stories into one.

Anderson and Fite go so far as to say that the wedding ceremony itself should more thoroughly ritualize this movement — from the family of origin to the beginning of a new family. Anderson and Fite have a point. More could and should be done. But the typical Presbyterian wedding ceremony does acknowledge this movement in certain ritualistic ways.

In the Presbyterian marriage rite, both sets of parents are asked to stand at an early point in the ceremony and to make promises in support of their children. Most of what happens during a wedding ceremony is important and filled with symbolism. But the moment when parents say publicly that they are letting go of their son or their daughter is particularly dramatic — filled with tension, sadness, relief, and even, occasionally, joy.

121

Tears are often a part of wedding ceremonies. I'm often amazed by the number of people who cry at weddings. Over the years, though, I've attributed most of the tears I've seen to the underlying theme of leaving. On the surface a wedding ceremony is mostly about cleaving, but the unstated purpose of a wedding is to make public the leaving. Sons and daughters don't cease to be sons and daughters, as I sometimes remind them in my wedding sermon, but something about the relationship with their parents comes to an end when a marriage begins. A new relationship between husband and wife begins, one that takes priority over the previous relationship between parents and children.

It shouldn't be surprising that a certain amount of grief would be connected to that change. But excessive sadness surrounding a wedding ceremony is a signal that something has probably broken down in the leaving-and-cleaving process.

In general, I'm sympathetic to the suggestions and insights that Anderson and Fite offer. In fact, I've occasionally made use of genograms in pre-marriage preparation. I remember one young man in particular who looked at his genogram and became consciously aware of a family dynamic that I don't think he ever really saw before. The men in his family tended to withhold their love from their children. They could establish loving relationships with their grandchildren and in some cases their great-grandchildren, but, in a pattern that stretched back as far as anyone could remember, fathers were not emotionally connected to their own children.

I remember that he and I talked for a long time about the implications of this insight, and I remember his desire to explore it more thoroughly with a therapist, but I realized that day — in a way I never had before — how important family-of-origin work can be as couples prepare for marriage. This young man was convinced — and I agreed with him — that he had some work to do before he and his fiancée would be able to achieve what they both wanted from their marriage. He certainly had some work to do before children were introduced into the relationship.

My reservation with the helpful work that Anderson and Fite have done is not about their suggestions for serious and intentional work on leaving before cleaving. My reservation comes from their suggesting that pastors be the ones to assist couples in this area. In my experience, most pastors don't have the skills or the training that Anderson and Fite have. Most pastors aren't therapists. This is not to say that pastors don't play a key role in helping couples with certain aspects of the leaving process. But when couples come to us who clearly have a number of serious "leaving" issues yet to solve, we are often ill-equipped to assist them.

I think a more balanced solution might be to see the work of leaving as a shared responsibility within the community of faith. Parents play a key role, of course, in assisting their children toward adulthood, but what about others? Pastors, Sunday School teachers, youth leaders — one of the responsibilities we all have in our work with children and youth is helping them to grow up and become adults. The challenge of this task is best met when we all participate in it.

Up to this point, I've framed most of the discussion about leaving in terms of family — partly because this chapter is about family, but mostly because that's the literal truth of Genesis 2:24. Actually, though, leaving comes in many forms, and very often these other forms of leaving are just as important for successful cleaving.

Successful cleaving often depends on a marriage partner's willingness to let go of a number of things — from a childhood church affiliation, let's say, to feelings for a previous marriage partner. I can't name all the possibilities, but maybe I can name a few that will illustrate the point.

In an earlier chapter I mention that spiritual compatibility in marriage may require one or both partners to leave behind a childhood denominational home. When a Catholic marries a Protestant, for example, it's often helpful if one partner or the other lets go of this identity for the sake of the marriage. Sometimes the letting go will have repercussions in the family of origin, but even in those cases where the family approves of the change, letting go can be a difficult and perhaps even traumatic experience. Successful leaving, however, will often enhance the quality of the marriage relationship.

In the case of a second (or third) marriage, sometimes successful cleaving requires one partner to finally let go of a previous partner. If a prior marriage ended in death or divorce, it's common for people to bring some residual feelings from that relationship into the new relationship. And very often those residual feelings can make cleaving difficult.

A man from my church made an appointment to see me shortly after he had married for a second time. His first wife had died, and he had remarried. Everyone was happy for him in this new marriage, and clearly he himself had found a new joy in his life. But, he said, he was beginning to realize that he had moved far too quickly. He didn't regret his new marriage, but he knew he hadn't taken the time to grieve the end of his first one. His new wife, for example, wasn't prepared to live in a house with a lot of reminders of that other marriage. But he wasn't quite ready to put all of those reminders away. For this man, cleaving to a new wife was made much more difficult by some inadequate leaving.

Another example that comes to mind involves a woman I know who spent a long period of her life as a single person before getting married. She was apparently a very happy single person with many close friends, and one of the perks of the single life, she said, was not having to check in with anyone before making a decision. Her new marriage was having its difficulties, she admitted, because she wasn't willing to leave *everything* about her previous life behind. Checking in with someone and being accountable at so many levels was a brand-new and in some ways frightening experience for her. For the sake of successful cleaving, though, I thought she needed to do some more letting go of her past life and behaviors.

Many of the wedding ceremonies at which I officiate these days involve blended families. The larger issue of blended families is a complicated one, and it requires far more discussion than I can give it here. But I do want to make this point. In these situations, either or both of the partners will bring children into the new relationship. This means that just about everyone involved — including the children — will be required to do some leaving or letting go. In order to make a new family work, everyone has to be willing to accept the end of a previous situation (perhaps perfectly adequate for them) and be open to the possibility of something entirely new.

Cleaving: Changing Definitions of What It Means

In previous chapters on love, power, and sex, I've already said a great deal about the nature of the marriage relationship. I didn't use the language of cleaving in those chapters, but that's really what I had in mind. Basically, I described what it means for marriage partners to cleave to each other. Cleaving can also be described as the development of true intimacy, which is the emotional work of marriage. When marriage partners cleave to each other — in other words, when they find intimacy together — they develop close physical, emotional, and spiritual bonds.

When cleaving is very, very good, when the bonds become deep and strong, marriages can sometimes result in what I have called a visible sign of God's grace — or what Genesis 2:24 calls "one flesh."

In this section I simply want to discuss family as it relates to cleaving. What exactly is the role of family in marriage?

I'm answering that question here — under the heading of "cleaving" — because for most of church history cleaving was really all about creating family. If you had asked Christian people prior to a half-century ago what cleaving meant to them, they would have assumed you meant the establishment of a family.

What's interesting — and very often confusing — is the way our view of marriage has changed and therefore how our view of family has changed as well. Most people today, including most *Christian* people, no longer think of marriage simply as a way to create a family. Marriage is now about love and companionship. As we saw in the chapter on sex, it's no longer about making babies. Today, having children and creating a family is no more than an option for marriage. It's no longer the purpose of marriage.

Something I came across in my research illustrates how much the world has changed. The ancient Egyptians didn't even have a word for marriage, but they did have another expression, one that referred to family. A man was said to "establish a household," and that implied a home which included offspring. The notion that a man and a woman could have a mutually satisfying relationship without children would have been unknown to the ancients.

A couple of years ago the *Chicago Tribune* ran a long feature story about childless couples titled "Just the Two of Us." Accompanying the story were pictures of couples who appeared to be uncommonly happy. They were shown in playful and happy poses — with no children in sight. The article also referred to some new organizations that have Web sites where couples in similar situations can meet and chat about their experiences.[1]

The text of the article explained in detail what the pictures already communicated — that there's a growing trend toward "child-free marriage" (the preferred term), and that this trend is due to a number of reasons. Among them are more satisfying career opportunities for women, worry-free birth control methods, the high cost of raising children, overpopulation and environmental concerns, and, last but not least, "a lukewarm interest in putting up with children 24 hours a day, seven days a week."

That last reason may sound a tad selfish, even at a time when children aren't the main reason for getting married, but one person quoted in the article — Tani Randolff, 35, of Fayette-

---

1. One of the most interesting I found was the ChildFree Association (www.childfree.com). Others include Childless by Choice (www.now2000.com) and No Kidding! (www.nokidding.bc.ca).

ville, Arkansas — rejects the selfish label. "Having a child just to satisfy your parents, to carry on the name, to leave your 'mark,' to save a marriage, these are definitely more selfish [reasons]," she says. "People should have children because they want them, not to fill a void somewhere."

As if to underscore the attractiveness of the child-free option, recent studies by Arizona State University have concluded that "no kid couples remain throughout their marriages as happy as pre-kid couples are before the babies start to come." On the other hand, couples with children, especially very young children, report a very low sense of marital satisfaction. If marriages survive the early years of child raising, marital satisfaction climbs gradually until the children leave home. And research indicates that marital satisfaction returns to its highest levels only after the children are out of the house.

Those are remarkable — if not totally surprising — observations. Susan and I waited until we were in our thirties to start a family, and we now realize what idyllic days we had together before our children arrived. Our children have enriched our lives in countless ways. We certainly have no regrets about bringing them into the world. But to say that our lives changed is an understatement.

It's hard to describe how much marriage changes when children are introduced into it. At the time Susan and I felt as though our world had shifted on its axis! And in a way it had. Instead of being focused exclusively on each other, we were focused primarily on our children. They demanded — and received — a great deal of our time and attention. Sometimes we found those demands to be taxing on what we considered to be the *primary* relationship: our marriage. And yet we always found the inner resources to work at both our marriage and the family we had created.

For most people — strange as this would have sounded to our grandparents — children get in the way of the physical, emotional, and spiritual intimacy of marriage. Sometimes, of course, they can bring couples closer by providing them with a shared focus on nurturing; often, though, they do not, as those university studies make clear.

In my chapter on sex, I concluded that our changing attitudes toward the role of sex in marriage (it now seems to be for pleasure more than for reproduction) raised confusing questions that Christians are still scrambling to address. On the subject of family, something similar seems to be happening. If children are no longer an essential component of marriage, that raises some confusing questions about the role of family — and even what properly constitutes a family.

Like the decision to get married, the decision to become a parent is probably best understood as a matter of vocation. It seems so clear to me that some people are called to be parents. Some people seem to have all the right gifts to be moms and dads. As I look around my neighborhood and community, I see people who seem to be doing a fine job of raising children. They have the resources, both material and personal, to make a real home for their children, and their children are thriving.

And it seems just as clear to me that other people don't have all the right gifts to be parents. Not all men and women seem to have what it takes to raise a family. That's clear to me when I look around and see people who seem to be seriously struggling as parents. I think it's important to remember that not all men and women should be expected to raise a family simply because they're married or because their reproductive equipment is in working order.

In my chapter on singleness, I urge that both marriage and singleness be thought of as matters of vocation. In other words, as people think about getting married, I believe they should try to discern, in a spiritual way, whether or not God is calling them to marriage. I don't have any kind of "test" to offer in this situation. Vocation is a spiritual matter that requires spiritual discernment — and a fairly high level of maturity. I wish that couples would use that same process to decide whether or not God is calling them to be parents.

In my own ministry, when I officiate at wedding ceremonies,

I no longer pray that the couples have children. Most wedding rites include a reference to children somewhere in the wedding prayer. In fact, the wedding rite I typically use has an entire paragraph about children in the wedding prayer, asking God to bless the marriage with children. But I no longer use it.

Half of all couples who get married at my church are . . . well, older. Let's just say that they're past child-bearing age. Sometimes older couples whose partners have died find love and get married again, but their children are often grown and out of the house. They have no plans to start another family.

There was a time when the church would not have blessed such marriages, when priests would have refused to officiate, but that day has passed. Marriage has come to mean something very different to most people.

It's possible to cleave together in marriage without having children.

Conclusion

It's not just our picture of marriage that's changed; our picture of family has changed as well. Television sitcoms of the 1950s portrayed idealized American families, consisting of a mom, a dad, and often two children. We saw those images so often that for most people they became icons.

Social scientist James Q. Wilson speaks for many people when he writes, "Marriage is an institution created to sustain child-rearing. The role of raising children is entrusted in principle to married heterosexual couples because after much experimentation — several thousand years, more or less — we have found nothing else that works as well."

But is Wilson right? Not according to my research. Based on my reading, the kind of family that Wilson describes — and the kind that politicians and religious leaders today hold up for us as the ideal — didn't really exist before the middle of the nineteenth century.

Historically, the concept of family is hard to define. The world in which the Bible was written had a sense of family that is very different from ours today, and it's one to which not many people would like to return. Those multi-generational, patriarchal households would be unrecognizable as family to most people today.

In the Roman world too, a family was very different from what we know it to be today. It consisted not only of legitimate children but also of adopted adults, slaves, and other dependents, all of varying ages. As one writer puts it, "Choice, not biology, made a *familia*" in Roman culture.

Even the 1950s model of family was in many ways the result of postwar economics, which found more people living in suburban settings and fewer on farms.

I sense that something similar to what happened in the Roman world is happening in our world. Family today seems to be determined less and less by biology, and more and more by decisions people make to be together. Recent research by the University of Chicago found that family units are also becoming much smaller, with two-parent families accounting for only 28 percent of the total in 1998 (down from 45 percent in 1972). The most common living arrangement in the United States today consists of two unmarried people living together.

To most pro-family advocates, these are discouraging statistics and indicators of an overall social breakdown. Many well-intentioned Christian people insist that something must be done. And so they're demanding that both the government and the church provide support to what they consider to be the ideal family unit.

I think the church should spend more time lifting up compelling and worthy ideals than legislating norms for the population. And I also think we need to remember that we're living in a time of dramatic change. In my chapter on covenant, I called it a time of "social revolution." But change and even social revolutions are nothing new in history. Our ideas about marriage and family are continuing to evolve.

Some truths endure, though, such as the one with which I began this chapter — leaving and cleaving.

Within the last half-century, Christian people have for the first time uncoupled the idea of marriage and family. Marriage is no longer about making babies. Sometimes people are called to be parents; sometimes they're not. Either way, happy, mutually satisfying, sacramental marriages are possible.

With this shift in thinking, the focus has turned to the quality of the marriage relationship — to the quality of our cleaving, we might say. Expectations for marriage have probably never been higher than they are today. In some cases, tragically, those expectations place impossible stress on marriages. More marriages than ever before are ending in divorce.

But there's good news too. Christian people want their marriages to be good. In fact, they want them to be more than good. Christian people want their marriages to be so good that God's grace becomes visible in them. Christian people today are working as never before toward the goal of becoming "one flesh."

Singleness and Marriage:
Unexpected Connections

Those who have the gift of celibacy from heaven, so that from the heart or with their whole soul are pure and continent and are not aflame with passion, let them serve the Lord in that calling, as long as they feel endued with that divine gift: and let them not lift themselves above others, but let them serve the Lord continuously in simplicity and humility. For such are more apt to attend to divine things than those who are distracted with the private affairs of the family.

Second Helvetic Confession, 1561

I know what you're probably thinking: A chapter about singleness in a book about marriage?

When I taught my adult education series on marriage, the topic for one of the classes was singleness. I included the topic without much thought. It just seemed to belong, though I didn't spend much time asking why.

Almost immediately after the opening prayer on that particular day, someone in the class raised a hand and asked, "Why are you teaching a class on being single? I thought the series was going to be about marriage."

I didn't sense irritation or disappointment in the question, only curiosity.

The question took me by surprise. With all of my careful preparation, with all of the reading I had done and notes I had taken, I had failed to ask myself an obvious question: Is singleness merely the flip side of marriage?

In my preparation for the series, I sensed that *something* should be said about singleness. What I hadn't considered was *why*. Which in and of itself is revealing. I am married, as I've noted earlier. I've been married for a long time — now into my third decade, in fact. Quite honestly, I don't spend much time thinking about what it means to be single. So, in a way, I was grateful for the question. It brought me up short. What does being single have to do with being married? What do Christians believe about singleness?

In the weeks after that Sunday-morning class, I thought a great deal about the question, and I came to see — with a greater appreciation than ever before — that for Christians being single and being married actually have a great deal to do with each other, as we'll see in this chapter. What I discovered, among other things, was that exploring singleness as a topic actually illuminated certain dimensions of marriage that I might otherwise have missed. Contrasting singleness and marriage, I have come to believe, can be a way of looking at each from a unique angle.

A month after Susan and I were married, we loaded a U-Haul truck with all of our earthly possessions — mostly an assortment of secondhand furniture and wedding presents — and moved to Iowa City, Iowa. I was going to begin a yearlong internship with a congregation there, and Susan was going to start law school.

Iowa City is a Big Ten university town, and so, not surprisingly, most of the members of the church where I was going to serve were related to the university in one way or another. Many were students. Many were young. And many were single. I'm guessing that there were more singles in that church than in the average American church.

A large part of my job description for the year was to work

with single, college-age youth and adults — both graduate and undergraduate students at the University of Iowa.

In the beginning I was thrilled. What a terrific job description! It's impossible to describe how excited I really was as the year began. There was my new marriage, of course, but I had also landed what I thought was my dream job in ministry. After all, I had just spent the first twenty-three years of my life as a single person. I thought I knew all about the single life.

What I didn't realize at the beginning of the year — and what the sponsoring church apparently didn't anticipate, either — was the almost inevitable awkwardness of asking a newly married pastor to head up the church's singles ministry.

Obviously I knew a lot about being a young, single seminary student, but what I didn't seem to recognize was the sheer variety of singleness there is in the world — and therefore the variety of experiences that single people have within their singleness.

And then, of course, there I was, showing up at nearly every social event, meeting, and spaghetti dinner with my brand-new wife, who was trying her best to be supportive of me and my work. Our "just married" status must have beamed out into the universe like a quasar.

As it turned out, I didn't know all that much about being single.

As the year went on, I began to see that we were a mismatch — not Susan and I, thankfully, but the group and I. We actually got along very well, and the group had its best year ever. So at one level, my work was satisfying, and I felt proud of my ministry. But when the year was over, I wrote in my summary report that I had been the wrong person for this ministry. It's possible, of course, that married pastors can be effective leaders for church singles groups, but by the end of my internship year I realized that I had been the wrong person at the wrong time for that particular group.

My presence was a weekly reminder that the members of the group were all somehow behind schedule, that marriage was actually the preferred state, and that singleness was not okay, except possibly as a brief, interim step before marriage. It's tough to admit, even now, but I think I was condescending to the group, even though that was completely unintentional. I just assumed all year long that they all wanted to be like me. And I tried very hard to be the perfect role model.

Looking back, I wish the group and I could have explored this issue together — my being newly married and their being single. It would have made for an interesting and helpful conversation. All of us might have learned something valuable.

Today I realize how much I didn't know about being single and how my perspective was terribly unhelpful for some members of the group. I am also much more aware of the subtle (and sometimes not-so-subtle) signals that a church sends to single people, letting them know in countless ways not only that they're different from married people, but also that they count for less.

Can the church do better? I think so. Much better. I know I can do better. To begin with, people of faith need a much better understanding of what singleness is. We need to remember what we believe about singleness.

What Does It Mean to Be Single?

I don't have the exact numbers for my church, but the number of single people who are members of my church is quite large, far larger than most members of my church realize. Because I live in a suburban, family-oriented community, I tend not to notice the single people around me. But they are there, and they are there in remarkable variety.

I read recently that 40 percent of all Presbyterians over the age of eighteen are single. In the same article I learned that half of all adults in the United States are single, with most of them living either alone or in single-parent households.

I'm guessing that those are surprising numbers to married people who live in communities like mine. Married people, especially married people with young children, tend to live near other people with a similar demographic profile, and because we do, we tend not to see those who aren't like us. It's entirely natural to see the surrounding culture as a reflection of our own lives. We assume that our neighborhoods and churches, and therefore our communities, are filled mostly with other married people, just like us.

On some level we recognize that this isn't the case. Single people are a large and growing percentage of the population. And yet so much of the church's focus, so much of the church's conversation, and so much of the church's program emphasis are on marriage, children, and family. Many of the single people I know report that they often feel invisible at my church. It's as though they *ought* to remain invisible, they say, until they get married and achieve the stature or respectability or whatever it is that goes with marriage. That's disturbing to hear, as you can imagine, and when they say it I can sense that their pain is real.

That's the not-so-subtle message the church — often *my* church — gives to single people. They're not welcome.

But that's not what we believe about singleness, is it?

Taking a brief look at church history will show us how some of our attitudes toward single people and singleness may have developed.

The Apostle Paul, in a sometimes-confusing and often-misinterpreted portion of his letter to the Corinthians, wrote to single people of faith that "it is well for you to remain as you are" (1 Cor. 7:26). In other words, he was saying, don't get married. That's Paul advice.

What some contemporary readers miss, however, is the unusual context in which Paul writes these words. Paul and his fellow believers thought that the end was near and that Christ would return at any moment to usher in his kingdom. It certainly never occurred to Paul, as he wrote these words, that people of faith two thousand years later would still be anticipating Christ's return.

136

So, most of what Paul writes in the surrounding verses — his instructions about marriage — ought to be read with this understanding. Don't get involved, he was saying. Don't entangle yourselves. The time is short. Focus all of your energy on getting ready to meet Christ when he returns.

That's the reason Paul says singleness is better than marriage. It's less complicated, given all that is about to happen.

Christ didn't return when Paul expected he would. But Paul's words about singleness nevertheless had a profound impact on the early (Catholic) church. Partly because of what he said, and partly due to other influences in early church history, the Roman Catholic Church began to lift up celibacy as an ideal state, a preferred way of life.

Married people came to be thought of as ordinary Christians, while first-class Christians were those who embraced lifelong singleness. Priests and those in religious orders (monks and nuns) were regarded as having a higher calling and a worthier spiritual commitment.

During the Reformation, Protestants emphatically rejected this two-tier view of spirituality, as well as the requirement that priests (or ministers) be single. Both Martin Luther and John Calvin, two of the best-known and most influential Reformers, were married. Calvin was never a Catholic priest, but Luther actually renounced his ties to the church and afterward was married.

Protestants attacked the whole notion of celibacy as a path to a higher spirituality, and instead they emphasized the importance of marriage. Christian growth, they rightly said, could take place in the context of home and family, not just in the monastery.

Some church historians have argued recently that Protestants — in their zeal to lift up the importance of marriage — may have inadvertently reversed the old two-tier model. If the Roman Catholics suggested in their teachings that singleness was to be preferred over marriage, then Protestants seemed to say that marriage was superior to singleness. And it's true that churches often act, plan, and budget as though marriage is of far greater importance than singleness.

While Protestants have never denied that singleness could be a calling, they certainly seem to assume that for most people singleness is not a lifelong state. I want to return to this idea of singleness as a calling. But first let's look at who single people are.

Is it possible to offer a definition of singleness?

As I mentioned, singleness comes in so many varieties that sometimes it's difficult to offer generalizations or even to see single people as a group. There are singles who are men, and there are singles who are women. There are young singles, middle-aged singles, and singles who are seniors. There are singles who are heterosexual, and there are singles who are homosexual. There are singles who live alone, and there are singles who live together with other people without being married. There are singles who have never been married, and there are singles who have been married — sometimes more than once. There are singles who have been widowed and singles who have been divorced. There are singles who are single by choice, though there are many more singles who say they would prefer to be married. There are singles who enjoy being single, and there are singles who are angry and resentful and lonely in their singleness.

Have I covered all the possibilities? Probably not.

I read somewhere that most people will be single at some point in their lives — in fact, that most people will live long stretches of their lives in singleness, either before or after marriage. And maybe for that reason alone the church should do a better job than it often does of ministry to singles.

Some of us may need that ministry some day.

Single People as Sexual Beings

I find it instructive to listen to the messages of popular culture regarding singleness. There are many different and competing voices, all claiming to speak with authority, but I find that a common theme is to describe singleness almost exclusively as a sexual matter. If there is a consensus about singleness in popular culture, it seems to be that singleness is mainly about sexual practice.

Old? Young? Single parent? Living alone? Male? Female? Those characteristics don't seem to matter nearly as much as what a particular person is doing sexually.

Laura Schlesinger, the host of a popular radio call-in show on "moral issues" — better known to her listeners as Dr. Laura — is one such voice. She recently passed Rush Limbaugh as the most listened-to radio host in the United States today, and by her own admission she has become increasingly vocal about America's moral situation.

Most listeners know that she regularly deplores live-in arrangements for unmarried couples. Her disparaging term for those arrangements is "shacking up." Sex before marriage, she says unequivocally, is morally wrong. And so, when Dr. Laura talks about what it means to be single, she invariably talks about sexual behavior — and very little else.

Dr. Laura is just one of many equally insistent voices in the American entertainment industry — television, movies, magazines, and so on. (Although Dr. Laura might consider her program a public service, it is very much a part of the entertainment industry.)

One popular and critically acclaimed television series is HBO's "Sex and the City." In each episode, four attractive and sexually active women, who live and work in New York City, describe their (mostly unsuccessful) relationships with men. If a television series can be said to make moral judgments, the moral judgment of this series is that sex before marriage is not only morally acceptable but pretty much a given among singles today. To be single is to be sexually active — and to talk about it extensively with other single friends.

A magazine appeared recently on the coffee table in my family room — a widely circulated, mainstream magazine aimed at young single women like my two teenaged daughters. The headline on the cover that grabbed my attention was "How to Have

Better Orgasms with Your Boyfriend — *Every Time!*" I found myself wondering if any other areas in male-female relationships
were really important.

To be single in our culture today, popular media seem to
say, is to be sexually active, to demand and find sexual pleasure
with multiple partners.

But isn't there more to singleness than a person's sexual behavior? Isn't there more to all of us — single *and* married — than
our sexual behavior?

What do Christians believe?

Much of what the church has had to say about singleness in recent years has also been about sex, mostly a response, I'm guessing, to the confusing voices we hear in popular culture. A few
years ago, for example, my own denomination — the Presbyterian
Church (U.S.A.) — adopted new language about marriage and
singleness for its constitution. According to the new language,
known as the "fidelity and chastity amendment," if you're going
to be married (defined as "one man and one woman"), you must
be faithful. If you're going to be single, you must be chaste. In
other words, no sex, except within marriage.

Those who can't comply with the rules will not be ordained
to any of the offices of the Presbyterian Church — elder, deacon,
or minister of the Word.

If people in my denomination were hoping for clarity on the
issue of morally acceptable sexual behavior, they certainly got it.
Here it was, finally — an answer that leaves no room for misun-
derstanding. Sex is for marriage only. And those who aren't married, for whatever reason, must not have sex. Singleness requires
chastity.

How about sex within a "committed relationship" consisting of two single people? No. The ruling was clear.

Though the new language disappointed some within the
church who were hoping for a less traditional, more nuanced response, there really was nothing new in what the church said.
The Presbyterian Church merely stated what most churches have

taught for centuries. What *was* new, I suppose, and what caught some church members off-guard, was to see the issue addressed in a legal or constitutional way.

The Presbyterian Church (U.S.A.) stands within a rich theological tradition — the *Reformed* theological tradition. Over the years, in fact, this tradition has been known for its intellectual rigor. One reason I am often proud to call myself a Presbyterian is that my church has contributed in substantial ways to the conversations surrounding most issues.

When we're at our best, we know how to think and act theologically. Here was an instance, however, where the Church declared itself constitutionally, not theologically. Legally, not pastorally.

No wonder some people were left unsatisfied with the decision. And no wonder the underlying tensions have not gone away. Several denominations and faith traditions continue to struggle with questions about human sexuality. If anything, the question is more urgent now than ever: What *does* our faith tell us about being single?

Single People as More than Sexual Beings: What Scripture Says

Let's begin where people of faith have always begun. What does the Bible say?

First, we believe that human beings, male and female, were created in God's likeness.

"So God created humankind in his image, in the image of God he created them; male and female he created them" (Gen. 1:27).

That's a core theological truth. Every person of faith, married and single, should be able to affirm that statement and know at least in part what it means. What does it mean for you that you were created in God's likeness?

141

At first, I admit, this might seem to be an unlikely — even unhelpful — place to begin, but actually, as we'll see, this particular truth is one of the best possible places to begin.

The *imago dei* is where theological conversations about human beings almost always begin. And this is what it means: Our primary identity is that we are created in the image of God. Which is extraordinarily good news, isn't it? This is what the creation story teaches us. This is a theological and spiritual statement about who we are, and its implications for our behavior and God's intentions for us are far-reaching.

One of the obvious implications of this biblical truth is that human beings are much more than sexual beings. We are sexual beings, to be sure, but we are so much more. We are also created to be loving, generous, hospitable, creative, self-sacrificing, forgiving, tender, persistent beings — to name only a tiny fraction of the characteristics we see in God. You can probably think of many more.

As image bearers, to use an old expression, God gave us a remarkable stature within creation. And so — to put it bluntly — reducing human beings to a single characteristic, a single quality, or a single dimension, as popular culture so often does, robs us of the full humanity God intended for us.

I am a sexual being, and so are you, but surely we are more than that — much more. That's what our faith teaches us.

Another implication of the *imago dei* is that we were created to be in relationship with each other. Just as God is a God-in-relationship (the three persons of the Trinity form what one theologian has called a "society of love"), so human beings were created to be men-and-women-in-relationship, whether married or single.

I think it's plain that human beings were intended to be in relationship to each other. We need each other, in fact, to grow toward personal and spiritual maturity. To deny significant and emotionally rich relationships to anyone is to deny what makes us human. Neither married people nor single people were intended to live isolated lives.

Second, God values both marriage and singleness.

Early in the biblical record, we read that God gave the first man and the first woman to each other in marriage. "Then the LORD God said, 'It is not good that the man should be alone; I will make him a helper as his partner.' . . . Therefore a man leaves his father and mother and clings to his wife, and they become one flesh" (Gen. 2:18, 24).

I have more to say about "leaving and cleaving" in the previous chapter. In this context it's enough to say that these words, because of their location in the creation story, have always had strong implications for us. They let us know early on that God values the marriage relationship between a man and a woman.

No surprise, maybe, but there it is.

And yet I find it more than just interesting to note that Jesus himself was single. There are a few biblical scholars who have raised doubts about this, but the general consensus over the years has always been that Jesus never married, that he devoted himself fully to his ministry, and that the only family life he knew was with his father, mother, and brothers. (There are no biblical references to sisters.)

Not only was Jesus himself single, but he chose as his friends both married and single people. During his ministry, Jesus made no distinctions among the people with whom he chose to associate based on marital status. From that we can infer that he makes no distinctions today.

As a single person, Jesus loved fully. In fact, Christian people have always believed that Jesus was unique among human beings in that he was able to love God and other people perfectly. More than that, Jesus was able to affirm sexuality without ever marrying or having sex with anyone. During his lifetime, Jesus had both male and female friends, he cared for and healed both women and men, and he gave his life freely for all. He was a model of God's inclusive, self-giving love.

All in all, Jesus' life was a strong affirmation of singleness. In a sense his life was a model of singleness.

Notice, however, what I'm not arguing. Jesus was single, but

God isn't holding up singleness as a *preferred* way of life. I think it's enough to say that in Jesus God was affirming singleness. Being married is good, but so is being single. The fact of Jesus' life strongly suggests that being single is — or can be — pleasing to God.

Here's an important issue to consider. The Christian tradition has long maintained that faithfulness within marriage and chastity within singleness have the paradoxical effect of freeing us, in marriage and in singleness, to express God's love more fully.

In other words, vows of faithfulness within marriage need not be an obstacle to love for others outside marriage, but can be experienced as providing the freedom to express love more deeply. And similarly, the church's historic position on chastity in singleness is rooted in the conviction that chastity encourages single people also to love more deeply.

A member of my church, a single woman, has helped me to see and understand this insight, and I am grateful for her help. Not long ago we had a conversation in which she told me that she has been able to develop several intimate, nonsexual relationships with both married and unmarried friends. Her commitment to singleness as a way of life has actually freed her, she has discovered, to love the people in her life in a way that might not have been possible otherwise.

As she and I talked, I came to see that it was true. Our own friendship has been an example of what she describes. Her stated desire to be single and her happiness with that status, in addition to my own commitment to my marriage, have made it possible for us simply to enjoy each other. We are freed, in other words, to love more deeply.

Kathleen Norris, a Presbyterian writer, had a similar experience when she lived among Benedictine monks and spoke with them about their vows of chastity. She describes this experience in her book *Amazing Grace*. At first, she says, she had doubts about their way of life, as many of us might. She wondered if it was possible to live fully as they were living.

But after spending an extended period of time with them,

she began to understand singleness — *their* singleness — in a new and much more appreciative way. Norris's words about celibacy and life among the Benedictines are among the most sympathetic I have ever read in Protestant literature: "I have been told by monks and nuns that hospitality is the fruit of their celibacy; they do not mean to scorn the flesh but live in such a way as to remain unencumbered by exclusive, sexual relationships. The goal is being free to love others, non-exclusively and non-possessively, both within their monastic community and without."

It's important to note that these monks and nuns are single by choice. All of them willingly entered into their religious communities. I am aware that this is not true of many of the singles I know. The monks and nuns are different from most other singles in that they view their vows of celibacy as part of their vocation or calling.

Which leads me to my next point.

Third, both singleness and marriage can be understood as specific vocations or callings.

"Let each of you lead the life that the Lord has assigned, to which God called you" (1 Cor. 7:17).

Regrettably, "vocation" is a word that has fallen out of use in Christian circles. Our talk about careers and what we want to do with our lives has crowded out the notion that God too may have plans for our lives, different from what we might want for ourselves.

Vocation is an important word for people of faith, and I believe that we should become re-acquainted with it.

Simply stated, vocation is what God calls us to do with our lives. Knowing God's call requires a high level of spiritual discernment — and possibly even the help of Christian friends or a spiritual director. On our own, some of us often cannot distinguish between God's voice and the many other voices we hear.

Let me ask you directly: What is your vocation? In other words, what is it that God has called you to do with your life? Do you know?

Most often, when Christians do speak about vocation, they speak about their work, but vocation can have other implications for the Christian life too. When people choose to follow a particular religious or spiritual tradition, for example, they are also responding to God's call in their lives. I am a Presbyterian, and I have embraced the Reformed theological tradition as my spiritual home. I would say that this tradition is also my calling or vocation. I believe I have been called to be the best Presbyterian I can be.

Similarly, I am married, and I believe that I am following God's call in my life by being married. And so marriage for me is as much my vocation as my career or my faith tradition. I have been called to be a husband. And just as I honor God by being a pastor and a Presbyterian, I also honor God by being a husband, the best one I can be.

Certainly not all people are called to be married. Some people, it seems clear to me, are called to be single. So it's appropriate, I believe, to think of being single as a vocation. But notice I'm not saying that everyone who's single is necessarily called to live in that state. It's important to acknowledge at this point that not all people who are single are single by choice. Some people may very well feel called to marriage, and in fact may earnestly desire to be married, but for any number of reasons marriage may not be in their immediate future. For them, I have found, singleness is not a calling but a burden. I know several people for whom this is a difficult and often frustrating situation. To be confident of God's call but not to be able to live it out is a source of pain for them. As a pastor I find myself at a loss for words when I talk about the subject with these friends. I have no answers. It is an instance of undeserved pain.

Still, I think it's true for a number of people that being single is what God is calling them to be. Some people, whether they know it or not, have been called to live life as single persons.

Just as people at an early point in their lives try to discern God's call for them in terms of career, I wish more people would spend time discerning God's call in this area. Of all the people who have come to me during my ministry to talk about getting married, not one person has ever started the conversation by saying, "I've looked for God's call in my life, and after a great deal of prayer and soul-searching, I now believe God has in mind for me to be a married person."

Most people, perhaps mistakenly, assume that God has intended for them to be married. Maybe a good question for Christians to ask themselves is this one: "As I look at the gifts God has given me, as I listen for God's voice in my life, am I being called to a life of singleness or a life of marriage?"

Studies show that most people — more than 90 percent — get married at some point in their lives. But maybe fewer should. Maybe more people are called to singleness than they sometimes realize. Maybe not everyone has the gifts necessary to be a good marriage partner. Maybe more people could begin to see that singleness can be and often is a rich, fulfilling, and satisfying way of life. Not an interim step before marriage, but a God-honoring way to live.

L. Gregory Jones, in a recent essay on vocation, writes that true vocation, beginning to do what God wants for us, actually "makes more of us" than we would otherwise be. He goes on to write that vocation also *asks* more of us than we would otherwise give.

I like that insight and find it both helpful and suggestive. In terms of singleness, maybe what it means is that single people who feel called to be single can be not just better people but better *single* people. Maybe a sense of vocation would encourage single people to live more intentionally in their singleness, to try to be the best single people they can be.

Maybe the church could also recover its pastoral and prophetic role in this area if it began to speak about singleness in all of its richness, variety, and possibility — instead of the legalistic way it has of late.

Conclusion

Clearly, all of us, both single and married, can benefit from a better understanding of singleness.

If you are married, what are some of the ways that you can begin to value singleness? Who are the single people in your life? You probably know more than you think you do. What are your relationships with them like? How could those relationships be better, richer, and deeper?

It's important for married people to remember that not all single people want to be "set up" with other single people. Some do, of course, but it's important to check first. And even more important, we need to check our own attitudes. What is it that lies behind our desire to "set up" the single people we know? Is it an unstated belief that single people ought to be married — like us?

If you are single, how do you understand your singleness? As a gift from God? As your vocation? Or does it seem more often like a burden, a difficult and frustrating way of life? How do you describe what it means to be single? What do you want your married friends to know about you?

Divorce: When Marriage Comes to an End

The Fuller community intends to respond to its divorced members with a compassion that in no way compromises our conviction. We believe God wills marriage to be permanent and and that he is deeply grieved when any marriage fails. We do not intend to alter this conviction. In compassion, however, we recognize that, in our broken world, it may sometimes be the case that people do end their marriages.

From Fuller Theological Seminary's
"Statements of Community Standards"

Not long ago my daughter came home from school with a question from one of her friends. "The Bible says divorce is wrong, doesn't it?" her friend had asked her. "I'd like to know what your dad says about that."

I wanted to know more about where the question came from, of course, and why it was being asked. But after exploring all of that, the question remained. My daughter wanted to know what the Bible really says about divorce because her friend was telling her that it was a sin.

Our family, like most families today, has been touched by divorce, and so I was aware that my daughter's question had a special urgency, even if it was unspoken.

What does the Bible say about divorce? For most Christians, a great deal is at stake in the answer to this question — not only our relationships with people we love but also our belief systems. After all, if the Bible is really our infallible guide to faith and life, which is what we say we believe, then what do we do with its many statements about divorce, most of which are plainly negative?

When I came to the topic of divorce and remarriage in my adult education class, the number of participants on that particular day increased noticeably, and the atmosphere was palpably subdued. I could feel it as soon as we started. Several church members, in fact, came that day even though they hadn't previously participated in the class. Of all the topics I had publicized ahead of time, this was the one they cared about the most.

In some ways this interest wasn't all that surprising, because we live in a culture of divorce. People continue to marry in increasing numbers, but they're also getting divorced in ever-increasing numbers. Whether we like it or not, more and more marriage relationships are coming to an end.

What do Christians believe about divorce?

As I discovered during the research I did for my class, people of faith have said and written a great deal about divorce over the years, but there is very little agreement about it — except perhaps that divorce is almost always a tragedy, a great sadness for everyone involved.

Relationships between men and women have had problems almost from the beginning. When Adam explains to God, in Genesis 3:12, that "the woman whom you gave to be with me" was the reason for his disobedience, we know that something has gone wrong in their relationship. Blaming our partner for our own failures is never a healthy sign in a marriage. But Adam and Eve's relationship wasn't the only one in biblical history to have problems.

Moses, in Deuteronomy 24:1-4, gives the people of Israel detailed instructions for ending their marriages. Broken relationships were apparently a sad fact of life even before God's people came to Mount Sinai.

Clearly, the Bible is witness to the brokenness of human relationships since the Fall. But just what does the Bible say about divorce?

An Interpretive Note

In response to difficult questions like this one, what I usually say is that we need to agree first on our interpretive methods. Finding one verse in the Bible that sounds not only applicable but authoritative, and then lifting that verse out of its context, is generally not the way people have read and interpreted the Bible over the years, at least not in my theological tradition.

Reading the Bible in that way, which is an all-too-common practice, actually dishonors the Bible and diminishes its power to speak to us. We believe that hearing God speak to us in the words of Scripture requires some serious effort on our part, some careful reading. Generally speaking, "the Bible says it, I believe it, and that's that" approach seldom yields the full richness and depth of biblical truth.

One rule for reading the Bible on the issue of divorce — and any other difficult issue, for that matter — is to read the Bible as a whole. In other words, what the Bible says in one place ought to be balanced and put next to what the Bible says about the same subject in other places. This is an interpretive method known as "reading Scripture in light of Scripture." On the subject of divorce in particular, I think it will be a very important method to follow, as we'll see.

Another rule for reading the Bible is to do the best job we can of knowing the situation and culture in which the words were written. Where it's possible, knowing something about the author also helps. For some issues, as a matter of fact, this interpretive principle makes all the difference.

As we've seen in the previous chapter, when we examined Paul's statements about singleness, we discovered that he was profoundly influenced by his understanding of the end times.

Paul wrote what he did about singleness because he assumed Christ would return at any moment. People who read Paul's words about singleness at that point in the Bible should know why he wrote what he did. Otherwise they'll seriously misunderstand what God is trying to say to us.

As we turn to the matter of divorce, one critical insight to keep in mind is that the men of Jesus' time considered it an important right to be able to get rid of women who didn't please them. Divorce was considered to be one of the most important rights a man could have. Women, it's important to note, had no similar right.

Furthermore, divorces were extraordinarily easy to get. One influential school of thought at the time (followers of Rabbi Hillel) believed that a man could divorce his wife "if she burned [her husband's] soup . . . or spoiled a dish for him." Rabbi Akiba took this line of thinking a step further and taught that divorce was acceptable if a man "should find a woman fairer than his wife."

A second school of thought (followers of Rabbi Shammai) was more restrictive, believing that divorce should be allowed only on moral grounds, such as adultery.

I found it fascinating to discover that Jesus' own disciples were clearly products of their culture. They too strongly valued their right as men to get a divorce. Matthew's Gospel includes a revealing scene in which Jesus answers a question from the Pharisees about divorce. We'll take a closer look at these verses later in this chapter, but for now it's enough to note Jesus' response. He makes it clear that he wants a far more restrictive understanding about divorce, allowing it only on moral grounds.

And so, later, the disciples follow up on what they've heard. "If such is the case of a man with his wife," they say in disbelief, "[then] it is better not to marry" (Matt. 19:10). As far as I know, this isn't the attitude of most men in our culture today, but we should remember that it was the prevailing attitude then.

A second critical insight to keep in mind is that in first-century culture a divorced woman had very few options, and none was attractive. A relative might be willing to take in a divorced woman, but her role in the household would ordinarily be that of a domestic servant. Remarriages to other men were sometimes possible, but they were rare and seldom happy. Such women were sometimes treated like "damaged goods." A final option for a divorced woman would be to choose prostitution as a way of surviving.

Unless we fully appreciate this background to divorce, I doubt that we can fully appreciate what Jesus has to say about it.

Much more could be said, of course, but these interpretive principles and first-century insights should be enough to get us started.

What Does Scripture Say?
Understanding Key Passages

There are at least four places in the New Testament where strong statements are made about divorce and remarriage. I think it's important to look at each one in turn.

Luke 16:18

Jesus' words in Luke 16:18 appear to be a bold and straightforward declaration that ought to settle the matter quickly: "Anyone who divorces his wife and marries another commits adultery, and whoever marries a woman divorced from her husband commits adultery."

A literal reading leads to a very clear conclusion: divorce *and* remarriage are both wrong. But is this what Jesus is saying?

Nearly all scholars agree that this saying of Jesus is actually an abbreviation of a saying that appears in longer form in Matthew 5:31-32 as part of Jesus' Sermon on the Mount.

As you may recall, these words occur in a long litany of sayings that have the same basic structure: "You have heard that it was said . . . but I say to you." In other words, Jesus is contrasting *his* views with those of Judaism.

In this case, the complete statement is, "It was also said, 'Whoever divorces his wife, let him give her a certificate of divorce.' But I say to you that anyone who divorces his wife, except on the ground of unchastity, causes her to commit adultery; and whoever marries a divorced woman commits adultery."

I think it's worth pointing out here that Jesus does see at least one circumstance that makes divorce acceptable. A marriage may come to an end on the ground of unfaithfulness, and this so-called exemption clause appears both here and again in Matthew 19, as we've seen. (Interestingly, the exemption clause doesn't appear in either Mark or Luke, but that doesn't lessen its significance.)

Dallas Willard, in his award-winning book *The Divine Conspiracy,* has an insight about these words that I think is worth considering. Willard's overall contention is that Jesus objected not to divorce in general but to divorce "as it was then practiced." So, when he reads Matthew 5:31-32, Willard hears Jesus saying, "Just because you've done everything legally — in other words, just because you've followed the law of Moses and given your wife the appropriate certificate of divorce — doesn't mean you've done right with regard to the relationship."

Those who sought a divorce, as it was then practiced, assumed that following the proper legal procedures made divorce acceptable, and Jesus vehemently disagreed. Life in the kingdom of heaven, Jesus was saying, requires something more from us, far more. Life in the kingdom of heaven requires us to go beyond the law.

To be thorough about this point, let's look briefly at one other place in the Gospels where Jesus seems to say the same thing, but actually adds a new wrinkle. In Mark 10:11-12, Jesus says, "Whoever divorces his wife and marries another commits adultery against her; and if she divorces her husband and marries another, she commits adultery."

What's remarkable about those words — do you see it? — is

that women could not, according to the law, divorce their husbands. And yet Jesus includes women equally in this charge: "If *she* divorces her husband . . ."

There's something else we should see here too.

A more literal translation of "she commits adultery" would be "she is adulterized." In other words, if a woman is divorced without a just cause, she is left in a just marriage. Therefore, remarriage for her would essentially be adultery. What Jesus is saying is that men who do this to their wives exploit and degrade them. The statement was meant not to prohibit remarriage but to condemn certain men for the way they treated their wives in divorce. Life in the kingdom of heaven isn't so much about keeping the letter of the law as it is about going beyond the requirements of the law.

In subtle but important ways, Jesus is looking out for and even promoting the welfare of women, who were among the neglected ones in his culture. He is also reminding the people around him that marriage is more than a legal agreement; marriage calls for something more from us.

Matthew 19:3-12

Let's move on to another passage — Matthew 19:3-12 (which is very much like Mark 10:2-12). The issue here is a question posed by the Pharisees. "Is it lawful for a man to divorce his wife for any cause?"

In response, Jesus makes a reference to Genesis and emphasizes God's intention regarding the lifelong nature of a marriage.

But the Pharisees persist with another question: "Why then did Moses command us to give a certificate of dismissal and to divorce her?" Jesus responds bluntly: "It was because you were so hardhearted that Moses allowed you to divorce your wives, but from the beginning it was not so. And I say to you, whoever divorces his wife, except for unchastity, and marries another commits adultery."

Most scholars agree that Jesus was arguing here against all the spurious grounds on which men were divorcing their wives. Even unchastity, he seems to say, does not *have* to mean the end of a marriage. It's certainly not a requirement that a marriage come to an end because one of the partners has been unfaithful, though most first-century males would have taken that position. (Remember Joseph's response when he discovered that Mary was pregnant.)

Jesus' point in these verses is that Moses *permitted* divorce in certain situations; he certainly didn't *require* it. And there's a difference.

Over the years Christians have sometimes understood these words to forbid divorce, and on the surface that's what these words appear to do. But a more careful examination, as we've seen, reveals that Jesus is after a deeper truth here. "It may be lawful for a man to divorce his wife," Jesus seems to say, "but that's not what God desires. God desires a permanent union." Jesus actually reaches all the way back to the Old Testament, to the first man and woman, and refers to God's desire for marriage.

1 Corinthians 7

The third passage is from a letter written by the Apostle Paul (1 Corinthians 7) to the Corinthian Christians. Paul discusses Christian marriage at length in this chapter, and essentially he echoes the words of Jesus, saying that husbands and wives should not leave each other but should work toward reconciliation.

Then Paul takes up an issue that Jesus didn't address. The issue, basically, is this: What happens if one of the partners in a marriage is a Christian and the other isn't? What makes this an especially interesting question is that it was a problem then, and, in my pastoral experience, I know that it continues to be a problem today. As long as Christians marry people who don't embrace the Christian faith, it will continue to be a problem.

Paul's answer is straightforward. Christians should not divorce their non-Christian partners: "If any believer has a wife who is an unbeliever, and she consents to live with him, he should not divorce her. And if any woman has a husband who is an unbeliever, and he consents to live with her, she should not divorce him" (vv. 12-13). There's always the chance, Paul writes, that the unbelieving partner could come to faith through the believing partner's faith.

But here Paul gets into even more interesting territory. He seems to make *an additional exception* to Jesus' rule on divorce. If the unbelieving partner "separates" or leaves the marriage, the believing partner, Paul writes, should not feel "bound" — as though he or she is still married. Notice that this applies equally to both men and women. In other words, the partner who is left should feel free to remarry.

1 Timothy 3:2; Titus 1:6

The last passages we'll examine here are also from Paul — 1 Timothy 3:2 and Titus 1:6. Paul states quite clearly that bishops (1 Timothy) and elders (Titus) should be "married only once" or be "the husband of one wife."

Over the years these verses have — wrongly — been used by churches and various Christian organizations to disqualify potential leaders from service. Very few — if any — Bible scholars today would accept this application of Paul's words.

For one thing, it's a distinct possibility that Paul was simply referring here to the practice of polygamy. Roman law prohibited having multiple wives, but it was still legal in first-century Palestine. Monogamy was the norm, but men were theoretically permitted, by Jewish law, to have up to eighteen wives. And so it may be that Paul was stating what most already believed to be right practice — that Christian leaders should be "married only once."

For another thing, there is evidence that some men in the Greco-Roman world had concubines, even though they were not permitted by Roman law. More than likely Paul was making his expectations absolutely clear: Christian men, especially those in leadership positions, should be pure and moral in their marriage and family relationships.

Here is one very important conclusion we can draw from this look at the relevant biblical passages about divorce: When Jesus talks about divorce, he doesn't forbid it absolutely. Instead — and this is a distinction we need to see — he makes it very clear that divorce is never God's intention for women and men in marriage. He answers our questions about whether or not divorce is permissible by speaking instead about God's intention or desire for married people.

And God's intention or desire for married people, as we've noted in previous chapters on covenant and sacrament, is that the marriage relationship will go deeper than any other human relationship, including that between parent and children. A marriage relationship can go so deep and be so profound that it can actually become a visible sign of God's grace.

This is why Jesus, in Matthew 19:6, quotes the words from Genesis about a man and woman becoming "one flesh." God desires that marriage be a permanent and indissoluble relationship.

Supporting Marriage in a Culture of Divorce

Since this is God's desire for us, doesn't it follow that all Christian people should feel a special concern not only for their own marriages but also for others who are in marriage relationships?

God takes marriage very seriously. Shouldn't we? What are the ways that we, as a church or as Christian friends, can support and encourage others in their marriages?

Whenever I marry a young couple, I typically ask their parents to stand at a very early point in the ceremony. While they're standing, with their son or daughter, I remind them that not long ago they too stood in a sacred place and made promises to each other, perhaps with their own parents looking on. I also point out that their relationship has been fruitful and has produced the son or daughter standing in front of them. This is, understandably, a moment of great feeling, and I tell them that they have every reason to feel love and pride. Finally, acknowledging that the parents have most likely given their blessings in private, I ask them to say publicly that they will bless this new marriage.

Here's the question I ask: "Parents, do you give your blessing to [the first names of the couple] and promise to do *everything in your power* to uphold them in their marriage?"

"Everything in your power" is quite a promise to make, but then most marriages require all the support they can get.

After asking the parents to be seated, I then turn to the congregation and ask them a similar question: "Will all of you who are witnessing these vows today do *everything in your power* to uphold [the first names of the couple] in their marriage?"

Again, it's quite a promise to make, but it's important, especially at a wedding ceremony, for people of faith to remember the depth of God's desire for us in marriage and the importance of communal support.

Fuller Theological Seminary in Pasadena, one of the largest and most influential seminaries in the United States, has actually adopted a statement on marriage that I quoted from at the beginning of this chapter. The statement calls all members of the seminary community — faculty, administration, board, students, and staff — to very high standards regarding marriage, including the obligation to support and encourage those in the seminary community who are married.

Here is one striking section of that statement:

> Sensitive to the fragility of any marriage, and to the fact that the price of fidelity to the biblical ideal is often paid in the hard currency of patient courage, Fuller Theological Seminary intends to do whatever it can to encourage and comfort those members of the community who walk the path of fidelity in lonely need and turbulent pain. It is concerned not only to

help people salvage their distressed marriages, but to be a community of support for all who strive to make their healthy marriages and their strong families even healthier and stronger than they are. The seminary expects that persons who are experiencing a troubled marriage will recognize the importance of this community of support and will make good use of seminary and other resources in their effort to bring healing and wholeness to their marriage.

This is a statement that many churches might consider adopting in some form for themselves. After all, if we believe all that we say about marriage, isn't it also our responsibility to provide the sort of environment where marriages can become all that's possible for them to be?

Popular culture may be pessimistic about marriage, but Christians are not. Hollywood may portray contemporary marriage as unhappy and destructive, but we know better. Marriage can be — and in many cases is — much more. It's our responsibility, then, to say what we know to be true. Marriage is worth preserving and protecting. Marriage deserves our time and care.

When the Bonds Break

God calls us into relationship and equips us with everything we need to make our relationships life-giving and life-affirming. But . . . we are seldom the people God has called us to be. Often our most serious failures come in the relationships that are most important to us.

All of us know couples who are divorced — and my wife and I are no exception. When Susan and I first moved to Wheaton, we came to know a particular couple very well. Or we thought we did.

On the surface they seemed to have a good marriage. We saw them communicate openly with each other. We heard their promises of fidelity. And we believed that their marriage was as

160

strong as any we had known. Over time our friendship grew, we socialized together, and our children developed friendships with their children.

A few years ago, to our surprise and disappointment, we discovered that all was not as it appeared. As it turned out, there had been problems in the marriage almost from the beginning. One of the partners moved out, serious issues were raised, and almost immediately accusations began to fly. It was ugly.

As Susan and I tried to support both of our friends, we found ourselves wondering how we could have missed the problems in this relationship. Worse, we found ourselves in conflict with each other about how best to respond. The divorce of our dear friends was tearing at the fabric of our own relationship, and we soon realized that we couldn't talk about our friends without being in disagreement with each other.

That divorce has been final for several years now, as final as divorces ever become, but the effects still linger, and the ripples are still felt through my church. Both partners have left the church, but both are still in the community, meaning that we continue to see each other occasionally.

Our meetings are awkward. I don't want to admit it even now, but I can see that our friendship will never be what it once was.

Is this something that God wanted — for them or for us? Clearly, it wasn't. Divorce is brokenness. And the feeling of brokenness continues. I don't know that it will ever go away.

In some ways it's too soon to reflect on my own role in what happened — or the church's role, for that matter. Could I have done something different? Probably. Could the church have responded differently? Undoubtedly. We made mistakes, painful ones. We should have been better than we were. And so we feel a sense of shame, a sense of failure.

From a pastoral point of view, divorce is probably the most difficult situation there is to deal with in the church, certainly the most difficult I've faced in my twenty years of ministry.

As a Presbyterian colleague, Joanna Adams, has put it, "Nobody knows what to do when a marriage ends. No one bakes a casserole or sends flowers. Nobody is happy about it really, least of all the two who concluded that of all the options available, this was likely the best one."

When members of my congregation are sick or facing surgery, we mention their names in worship and invite prayers for them. We start prayer chains and let as many people know as we can. A network of love and care seems to appear automatically. We seem to know what to do.

When members of my congregation are in crumbling marriages, however, our responses are anything but instinctive. Too often we appear helpless and act as though we're paralyzed. Even though prayer would be as appropriate as it is in a situation of illness, we work hard to keep the identity of those involved confidential.

Who are we protecting — those in difficult marriages or ourselves? Whatever the answer, many church members suffer the pain of separation and divorce without the love and support of their church family.

Clearly, this shouldn't happen. When marriages come to a tragic end in divorce, Christians have a responsibility to show compassion and love. When churches turn away from members whose marriages have ended, they unnecessarily multiply the hurt and pain involved.

Sometimes faithful church members, in their attempt to honor God's intention for marriage as a permanent and lifelong covenant, have in the process passed judgment and singled out divorced people for particular shame. These people forget what the Bible says in another place about how "all have sinned and fall short of the glory of God" (Rom. 3:23).

No one is perfect. Which begs the question: Is divorce a sin?

For some Christians, I've come to realize, this is an important question to ask. I'm not always sure why, but it deserves an answer simply because it is asked so often. I sometimes hesitate to give an answer, though, because many times the divorced person already feels an overwhelming sense of shame or failure. In my opinion, it doesn't do much good to say the obvious.

Christians believe that any behavior or conduct outside of God's intention for us is sin. To put that another way, sin refers to the way things are in the world, and things in the world today definitely aren't the way God intended them to be. So, in this sense, of course divorce is sin.

I suppose that we could think of instances in which one marriage partner would be considered justified in seeking a divorce and therefore innocent. Situations of abandonment, for example, come to mind. But Christians have always emphasized that sin is pervasive. No one, our theology teaches us, is completely innocent. We are saved and sinners, both at the same time.

Here's another point that ought to be made. Just because some married couples have managed to avoid divorce doesn't mean that their marriages are therefore free from sin. I can think of situations where the marriage is intact but is hardly what we could call life-affirming and God-honoring. Not all marriages are what God intends them to be simply because they have endured.

Several times in the last few years, my own church has received into membership women and men who have gone through painful divorces and who have left their previous church home. They have come to us to start over, to find a place of safety and a place of grace. While I'm glad for and proud of my own church's warmth and hospitality in these situations, I grieve the circumstances that have made such painful moves necessary.

The end of a marriage can be a time for church members to respond redemptively, to assist divorced people down the sometimes-long road to new life and hope.

Could Christian people begin to take up that cause?

If broken relationships are an inescapable fact of life, isn't there a way to divorce that is more consistent with what Christians believe? Isn't there a way to end a marriage that encourages cooperation, civility, and even healing?

I believe there is, but very few Christians seem to know about it. And fewer still seem to take advantage of it.

Many Christian couples come to the difficult conclusion that divorce for them is an unavoidable last resort. But that's rarely the end of the matter. The decision to divorce is typically just the beginning of more pain, more fighting, and more heartache.

In our country's legal system, the usual manner of ending a marriage is in litigation, which by its very nature is often contentious. Even couples who agree going into the divorce to be fair with each other can suddenly find themselves at odds, simply because the courts put them in that position. Each finds a lawyer, and then . . . well, the outcome is rarely a happy one.

There is another way, and I wish more Christian people would choose it. That way is mediation.

Sometimes people wrongly assume that mediation is a way of healing a marriage. It's not. Mediation is actually a way of *ending* a marriage, but without litigation — and the contentiousness that too often goes with it. Mediation brings couples together with a third person who is trained to remain neutral and to find ways to resolve conflicts. Those conflicts can range from child custody to the division of assets.

Most couples who choose mediation are advised by a lawyer at some point in the process, usually to make sure the settlement agreement is fair and legally sound. But — and this is the key point — the agreements are made together by the divorcing couples.

Data is in short supply because mediation is still relatively new, but early studies show that divorces resolved through mediation are far better for the children involved — and in many instances far better for the couples involved. Many court systems are beginning to make mediation a mandatory first step for couples going through a divorce.

With open conflict avoided, most couples can focus their energies on the issues that really matter. They begin the process of cooperation, if not for themselves, then for the sake of their children.

Mediation may not be the right choice for everyone, but if

we're looking for a Christian view of divorce, isn't it about time for mediation to be more widely embraced?

How would your divorce — or the divorce of someone you know — have been different if mediation had been used?

Conclusion

Divorce is a painful reality, both inside and outside the church. But I am heartened by the number of Christians I know who are still in their marriages.

I sometimes ask couples who have been married for fifty years or more what the secret of their enduring marriage has been. Most shrug their shoulders and say that it just happened. They were married, they worked, they had children, they had grandchildren, and then one day they woke up to find that fifty years had flown by.

Some of the couples I talk to feel as though they ought to say something profound or wise in answer to my question, and so they tell me about the hard work they put into their marriages. And I believe them. My own marriage has not yet endured for fifty years, but I know the work that has already been required over the years. I can begin to imagine what fifty years of marriage will require from me.

And yet, the real reason for marriages that endure is probably something more, something deeper. There are the obvious reasons, like good health, of course. Both partners have to be healthy enough and live long enough for a marriage to last. Then there is maturity — the capacity of both partners to make and keep a promise. But in the end the most important factor, I have come to believe, is a lot harder to name or describe.

It is, in a mysterious way, the grace of God.

A long-term marriage, more than anything else, is a gift. We don't earn it. We seldom deserve it. And not all of us receive it. But for those of us who do, it can only be described as a gift from God.

Ten Things I Wish Someone
Had Told Me about Marriage

The twelve most important words in a marriage: "I am wrong,"
"I am sorry," "Please forgive me," and "I love you."

Cliff Barrows, Christian singer

Here are ten things I wish someone had told *me* about marriage (not that I would have listened).

I say these things, in one way or another, to just about every couple who wants to be married at my church. I don't expect that these couples heading for marriage will actually hear any of this, but I believe these are important bits of pastoral advice. The first nine are more practical than theological, but they're based on years of both pastoral and personal experience.

1. This is going to be a lot harder than you think it is.

When I first thought about getting married to Susan, I confess that I wasn't all that realistic about how difficult marriage would be. I knew all about our financial situation, of course, which included several student loans, a new car loan, and very few assets. I could see the years of graduate school that were looming ahead of us. And I could anticipate a few other obstacles too. But what I didn't really seem to grasp was how much work would be involved in actually living with another person, achieving the emotional depth and intimacy we both said we wanted.

I wish someone would have told me how hard marriage was going to be.

Charlie Alcorn, a clinical psychologist whose insights I mentioned in a previous chapter, sometimes tells couples he sees in therapy that the degree of difficulty in married life, on a scale of one to ten, would be about fifteen. My sense is that fifteen is actually a low number, but it makes the point.

To illustrate exactly how difficult marriage can be, Charlie asks couples to think of it as a game. It's a game, he says, between two players who aren't highly proficient, on a playing field that's not level, with boundaries that are never defined, with no established rule book, and with no referee. In other words, the chances of running into serious difficulty are very, very high.

Why then do so many couples think marriage is going to be easy?

I think it's the endorphins. I don't claim to know exactly how it works, but apparently, when we fall in love, the body releases a chemical that gives us a feeling of well-being and contentment, even euphoria. The feeling tells us everything is right with the world. It's quite a good feeling, to be honest about it. And extremely powerful too. I know because I've had it.

The couples who come to me to plan a wedding ceremony are usually smitten with each other. They're intoxicated with the feelings of love they have for each other. They smile a lot, and they seem almost giddy with the thought that they're in love. Sometimes I think they're in love with the idea of being in love. The gland or organ or whatever it is that secretes the endorphins has been working around the clock, doing its scary work. Often the couples I see aren't thinking very clearly or making the best possible decisions. There's a reason for the old expression about falling "madly in love."

As we continue meeting together, I become aware that these couples are going to get married — with or without my help. They are moving toward each other at what seems to be the speed of light. If I have a concern about their relationship or the wisdom of their decision to marry each other, and then express that concern to them, the results will be predictable. There will be a collision. And I know from experience what many of them will do. Most often they'll simply find another church down the street from mine where they *can* be married — hassle free. Many of my colleagues in ministry have had a similar experience.

Getting in the way of couples who are determined to be married, generally speaking, is a risky place to be.

My church has a policy that's designed to avoid situations like these. Rather than getting in the way, we do our best to equip couples, to give them all the tools we think they'll need to succeed in their life together. In addition to meeting with me, we require them to take a communication course for couples, offered either at our church or at the pastoral counseling center our church supports. It's an excellent course, very realistic about the daunting task of communicating effectively with another human being. I've taken it, and so have several staff members at my church — to enhance our own ability to get along with each other.

The couples who come to us can hardly believe that *any* course is going to be necessary. For others, maybe, but not for them. They are, after all, probably the best communicators in the *entire history* of communicating couples.

"Why?" they ask me. "When we first met, we stayed up *all night* just talking with each other. There isn't *anything* we can't talk about together."

I believe them, but hold firm. "Please take the course anyway," I say. "Marriage is going to be a lot harder than it looks to you right now." They look at me as though I don't understand, as though I haven't yet grasped the depth of their love for each other, but most often they take the course.

In my chapter on power, I mentioned the desire Susan and I had at the beginning of our relationship for equality and mutuality. We wanted our partnership to be a fifty-fifty proposition. My father-in-law tried to discourage that kind of thinking and told us that most days marriage would be a sixty-forty proposition at best. In other words, what I heard him say was that you have to be prepared to give more than you take.

As it turns out, he was right. Virtually every study of long-term marriages in which couples report a high level of satisfaction and contentment demonstrates that both partners in a marriage have to be willing to give more than they get back.

In the long run, the giving and the taking *may* balance out, but there's no guarantee. Going into marriage, both partners have to be willing to give. And give. Even when they don't feel like it. *Especially* when they don't feel like it.

Now that I think about it, someone *did* try to tell me that.

2. Maybe the worst possible reason to get married — or pretty close to it — is that everyone else you know is getting married.

If that's how you're feeling, please give some further thought to your desire to be married.

If you live in a community like mine, I can only begin to imagine the pressure you must feel to be part of a couple. My community is about as couple-oriented as it's possible for a community to be. Everywhere you look — or so it seems — there are couples doing couple-like things. They're holding hands, talking with each other, laughing, sharing a meal, shopping together, going to the movies. In my community I almost never see a person sitting alone in a restaurant or a movie theater.

I sometimes wonder if I would have the courage to do it myself. My guess is that I wouldn't.

One of the places in life where people very often feel intense pressure to be in a relationship is college. College often feels like a greenhouse for romance. All the conditions seem to be right for couples to start pairing up with each other. To put it bluntly, the selection and availability of potential mates are probably higher on a college or university campus than just about anywhere else.

So, if you're in college, and all of your friends appear to be matched up and are talking about "setting the date" and are actually buying rings . . . well, you're going to feel pressured to do the same.

Don't do it. At least not because everyone else is doing it. That's a terrible reason to get married, and yet that's exactly what happens to too many people.

Not long ago I was sitting with a groom just before his wedding. Actually, I was the one who was sitting, and he was pacing. It was a second marriage for him, and he was in a reflective mood — as reflective as it's possible to be in those few minutes before a wedding ceremony. He told me about his feelings just before he was married for the first time. His best man and ushers were all fraternity brothers, and all of them were getting married that summer too — or else they were in the "advanced planning" stages of their relationships. He said that it felt as though he was being swept along by a powerful current. He didn't know he had the power to stop it, or even that it might be a good idea to stop it. He thought that getting married was what he ought to be doing, even though it didn't feel right.

His first marriage didn't last long. He and his wife had no children, but they had many regrets.

Moving toward marriage is not an Olympic event. There are no awards for the fastest walk down the aisle. So, slow down. If marriage is right for you, it will happen.

3. Marriage is not a cure for loneliness.

It's a bad idea to get married if you think your loneliness will go away once you're part of a couple. Believe me when I say that if you've got a hole in your heart right now, you may very well have a hole in your heart after you're married too.

In my experience people who are lonely before a marriage are going to be lonely *in* a marriage.

When I was a seminary student, I remember feeling very lonely. I was still single, and Susan was hundreds of miles away, having decided to work for a year before starting law school. I lived alone, and my Greek and Hebrew textbooks sometimes seemed like my only friends. I was certainly spending more time with them than with anyone else. The many late-night, long-distance telephone calls with Susan didn't do much to cure what I was feeling. If sending e-mail and chatting on-line had been options back then, I don't think they would have done much for me, either.

When we were finally together, I was thrilled, more so than I can adequately describe here. But I eventually made an important discovery. Mere physical proximity to another person is not necessarily a cure for loneliness. What I wanted, as it turned out, was intimacy — a deep emotional and spiritual bond. You can be with another person twenty-four hours a day, seven days a week, and not have intimacy with that person. Intimacy, I learned, is the emotional work of a relationship. Being together is a helpful start, of course, but there's no guarantee that intimacy will follow.

So, if you're single and lonely, your problem may not be your marital status.

4. Don't marry someone who will be "good for you."

Take my word for it. He won't be. Or *she* won't be.

If you're wounded in any way, don't marry your healer. If someone you know has been good for you, has helped you in some way, has opened up a whole new world for you that you never knew was there, or has simply been with you through a difficult time in your life, thank him — or her. Find a way to show it. Be grateful.

But please don't marry that person.

Why not? Because if you do, you'll both wake up one morning and realize what the relationship was based on. It wasn't mutuality. And at that point the relationship will be over. Or pretty close to it.

Here's my advice: If you're wounded, wait until you're well before you partner up with another person. If your life is incomplete, don't expect a marriage partner to fill in all the blank pages. You'll save yourself and that other person a lot of pain and disappointment by recognizing this.

Susan was good for me in many ways. She helped me too. At some point in our dating the thought probably crossed my mind that she could make my life better than it was. But I'm convinced that, if that had been the basis of our relationship, we wouldn't still be married today.

5. Don't marry someone with the thought that you're going to change something about him or her.

If you're thinking about getting married to someone, and in the back of your mind you're thinking that maybe you can change him or her, forget it. Even if it's something small — an annoying habit, let's say, or a tiny character flaw — don't do it.

People do change. And they change in miraculous ways, as a matter of fact. My faith tells me that the gospel has transforming power in our lives, and my experience has shown me that it's true.

But marriage is not a home improvement project.

In my chapter on love, I describe marriage as a school for character. I didn't use those words, but I suggested that marriage is a place where profound personal and spiritual growth can occur. In marriage our partners sometimes help us to discover parts of ourselves that we didn't know were there, both good and bad. They challenge us to grow in areas where we never expected to grow.

My point here is different.

Going into a marriage with the intent to change, fix, upgrade, polish, or rehabilitate your partner is always a bad idea. Trying to change someone, in fact, is a barrier to intimacy.

6. Early on in your marriage you must learn to say "I'm sorry" — and mean it.

Forgiveness within a marriage relationship is one of the ways we discover love and intimacy and depth, but forgiveness is usually easier when the partner who needs it is genuinely contrite and can own up to his or her failures and shortcomings.

I ask for forgiveness (and receive it) more often as a married person than I ever did as a single person.

172

7. Seriously consider remaining single.

Not everyone is capable of being a good marriage partner. Or, to put that another way, not everyone has what it takes to be happily married. Marriage really is a calling, a vocation, more than I ever imagined it was, and if you're not called to it, marriage could be a disaster for you — and also for the person you marry.

Singleness, on the other hand, is — or can be — a good and worthy way to live. From a faith perspective there is nothing second-rate about it. Most of the single people I know have deeply satisfying, emotionally rich, and intimate relationships with other people. You don't have to be married to find intimacy.

As I pointed out in my chapter on singleness, some people are called to be single. For them it can be a valid, God-honoring way to live.

Maybe you should give more thought to it than you have.

8. Treat your marriage partner like a gift from God — and as with all of God's gifts, never, ever take this particular gift for granted.

Gary Smalley is a psychologist who has written several books about marriage and has offered marriage workshops for couples throughout the world. He's a Christian too, and I believe he's done a good job of integrating psychology and theology.

One of his first insights about marriage — and one he continues to write and talk about — is the need to *honor* our partners.

Wives especially, he says, need to know that they are valued and cherished by their husbands. According to him, it's the primary need that women have within a marriage. They want to know that their husbands regard them more highly than anything else in their lives. (A husband's primary need, according to Smalley, is to be respected, to be considered adequate and competent.)

Very few couples promise in their marriage vows to "love, honor, and obey." Those words were a part of the standard wedding ceremony at one time, but they aren't anymore and haven't been for some time. Still, in popular culture it's these words that people usually associate with church wedding vows, and, not surprisingly, it's the word "obey" that they ordinarily object to.

I have no desire to go back to the "love, honor, and obey" formula for wedding vows, but we've lost something by no longer promising to honor our partners. We've lost something important in a relationship if we neglect to honor each other. Honor is the attitude that God wants from us in response to all of creation, but it is essential to have honor within our primary relationships. Honor includes a sense of wonder and awe — in other words, the capacity to be moved by how remarkable and unique your partner really is. When your partner walks into the room — even after twenty, thirty, forty, or more years of marriage — you need to be able to respond with a "Wow, isn't she something! I can't believe I'm married to someone as terrific as she is."

Honor is more than delight and admiration, though that's a very good start. It also includes a dimension of respect, knowing and being attentive to the needs and boundaries that our partners describe for us. When we honor the person we're married to, we regard that person's needs as being at least as important as our own.

In a study of more than three hundred couples who described their marriages as happy and successful, researchers Jeanette and Robert Lauer asked all of the couples to rank thirty-nine statements in the order of their importance. The statements covered all aspects of the marriage relationship, from sex and money to goals in life and attitudes about marriage in general. Men and women responded separately, with no knowledge of their partners' choices. The results were surprising — at least at first glance. On further reflection, though, the results made sense. Couples who believe they are in happy marriages are in general agreement about what makes them happy. In fact, the ranking of the first seven statements about marriage was exactly the same for both men and women.

I've included the top fifteen responses in an appendix, so you can compare both the similarities and the differences men and women have as they reflect on the components of a happy marriage. But for my purposes here, notice that four of the first seven have to do with a sense of honor and respect. Remember that both men and women rank the following responses in the same order:

- My spouse is my best friend (first).
- I like my spouse as a person (second).
- We agree on aims and goals (fifth).
- My spouse has grown more interesting (sixth).

When we no longer see our partners as the gifts from God they are, our marriages are in trouble. Honor, gratitude, appreciation, wonder, delight, and respect are all crucial components of a happy and successful marriage.

9. Accept conflict as an inevitable part of human relationships.

I know couples who don't fight. They don't fight because they've given up. They're tired of fighting, and they've agreed to a truce. They keep their distance from each other, and they glare at each other across a demilitarized zone. But they're not fighting.

I know other couples who don't fight. These couples appear to have healthy and happy marriages — and yet, remarkably enough, they never fight.

Such marriages are rare. They occur, but not very often. For most of us, occasional conflict is going to be part of the relationship. We're not perfect people, we don't always want the same thing at the same time, and marriage is difficult by any measure. So, for all these reasons and more, conflict is going to be inevitable.

But — and this is my point — it doesn't have to mean the end of the relationship. The marriage is not over because you're fighting. A single disagreement or even a string of disagreements is not a reason to consider the marriage finished. Studies of happy and successful marriages report both good times and bad times in these relationships.

On the other hand, conflict is almost always a signal — of something. Fighting is a clue that you need to pay attention. Usually something needs to be done.

If the fighting typically leaves one of the partners feeling hurt, defeated, demeaned, even abused, that's a signal that something isn't right with the relationship, and help is required. If the fighting is always about the same issue, that too may mean that you should be taking a careful look — either at the issue you're fighting about or something deeper, possibly an underlying problem. If one partner fights while the other partner withdraws or refuses to enter into the conflict, that's an important issue too, and it probably ought to be explored. Sometimes passivity can be very powerful, but often in a destructive way. Our refusal to fight doesn't always mean we're right and the other person is wrong.

Often couples need to learn to fight fair. Sound odd to you? Maybe it does, but it's true. If conflict is going to be inevitable within a marriage, then certain rules need to be agreed on — and observed. In boxing, there are penalties for "low blows." When marriage partners fight, there can be "low blows" too, even if no points are taken away.

In fact, that raises another important point. In a marriage no one should be keeping score. It's not a contest with winners and losers. What's at stake is always the marriage.

I think there is such a thing as healthy conflict. And it's best if marriage partners learn how to "fight fair" early in the relationship. If they need help developing healthy patterns of resolving differences, they might want to consult with a therapist.

10. Don't marry someone unless you're spiritually compatible.

I find that this is the least popular piece of advice I give to a couple before they marry. When I raise the issue of spiritual compatibility, I usually get a look that says, "You really don't get it, do you? Our love transcends all of that."

And it's true. If you're in love, you really do believe, with all your heart, that you can overcome *any* obstacle. And for some reason, religious differences are perceived to be the least serious of potential marital obstacles.

In my experience, as I've mentioned in an earlier chapter, they're not.

It's not enough to share a few interests or hobbies with your marriage partner. It's not enough to be able to talk together about any subject. It's not enough to have a strong physical attraction to each other. To have an enduring marriage, it's essential to build on a common spiritual foundation. And here I'm referring to more than specific religious beliefs, though that's an essential part of it. By spiritual compatibility, I'm referring more broadly to being in agreement about certain core convictions and values, having a set of shared beliefs about life and its meaning, and believing that marriage itself is sacred.

In the Lauer study of happy marriages that I referred to earlier in this chapter, both men and women ranked "marriage is sacred" as the fourth most important reason for what has kept their marriages going.

Marriages — good marriages — *are* sacred. They're object lessons in God's grace.

Making a Covenant

My twenty years of pastoral experience tell me that couples in general apply themselves in almost feverish ways to the relatively insignificant details of getting ready for the wedding day, while they forget just about all of the important aspects of their future — such as their family relationships, the way they communicate with each other, and their finances, to name just a few.

I don't have any particular nostalgia for the era of arranged marriages. I'm glad, as a matter of fact, that my parents played little or no role in finding a bride for me. They sometimes offered opinions about the girls I dated, but I always assumed that the decision about a marriage partner was going to be mine. Even so, at least one dimension of the old arranged marriage practice is sorely missing today: frank conversation about important issues *prior to* the wedding.

As I picture it, families of long ago would get together and have serious, Camp David–style negotiations, all in an atmosphere unclouded by romantic love. They would talk about money, housing arrangements, employment, transfers of wealth, and more. Children and faith issues were probably not difficult areas, and in most cases assumptions were probably made about these and other matters. Still, in my imagination at least, most of the important issues were addressed *before* the wedding — leaving couples with the comparatively small matter of getting along with each other.

I don't sense an imminent return to this method of entering into marriage, nor am I advocating a dramatic change in our current marriage customs. But I do think we've lost something. Most couples could enter into marriage more thoughtfully and deliberately than they currently do. Most couples are willing to admit — years later — that they did little or nothing to get ready for their lifetime together.

In my chapter on covenant, I mentioned a couple I married named Laurie and Chip who approached their marriage in such a refreshingly different way — refreshing in the sense that it was intentional and deliberate.

To them, writing a mission statement for their marriage seemed like a natural approach to take. They were intrigued by Stephen Covey's book *The Seven Habits of Highly Effective People,* as I mentioned, and they had already written personal mission statements for themselves. So they decided to take a weekend together and spend all of their time focusing on what their life together would be like, what their mutual hopes and dreams looked like.

A mission statement is one way to begin thinking about marriage as a covenant relationship. Of course, not every couple will feel comfortable with this approach, but I think it could work for many couples. And it's never too late to start. (In fact, one of the advantages of the marriage mission statement is that it can be written at any stage of marriage, even when children have entered the picture. As Covey himself suggests, *family* mission statements, in which children are also included in the conversation, can be very valuable. Take a weekend retreat with your family, he says, and write your statement. I think that's a wonderful idea, but again, it may not be right for everyone.)

I'm including here a copy of the statement Laurie and Chip developed in order to give couples an example of what can be done, and I'm grateful to Laurie and Chip for their willingness to share their hard work in this way. When I asked them if I could reprint it here, they agreed without hesitation. Their own copy, done in calligraphy, hangs in their bedroom as a daily reminder of what they believe and have agreed to.

They made it clear that they're sharing their statement to be helpful to other couples, not to imply that their way is the best way of getting ready for marriage. And their statement is only an example of what they believe to be important — nothing more. Other mission statements will surely look and sound different.

Here's what Laurie and Chip wrote together:

We believe that God created marriage to be a lifelong commitment to one another and a reflection of God's love for the world. We believe that we are God's gift to one another, as Adam and Eve were given to each other in order to help one another. As God cleaves us together in marriage, He unites the three of us, forming that strong cord of three strands.

We believe the foundation of our marriage should be kindness, compassion, forgiveness, selflessness, and unconditional acceptance. In living life according to those principles, we will look to the person of Jesus Christ as our model and companion. Together we will strive to reach the full potential of God's purpose for our lives.

We will make the time to listen to one another; encourage our partner to stretch, grow, and take risks; and support each other in all our endeavors. Though God has bonded us as one flesh, we will respect our differences, learn from each other's strengths, and support our partner's weaknesses.

We have spent the first part of our lives growing and maturing as individuals. Now we are ready to begin life together as a couple, and we look forward to our marriage continually growing and our love maturing.

We believe God's charge to us is to be visible Christians, always doing what is right in His eyes. We want so much from our marriage and for each other, but also we realize we need to keep perspective; take the time to enjoy life; and to have fun and laugh.

Laura Fuller and Chip Bevier
October 15, 1994

I like what Laurie and Chip have done, but I have a further suggestion — an outline for the conversation that ought to take place between brides and grooms before they get married. This conversation could definitely help shape the mission statement.

Todd Outcalt, in a book called *Before You Say "I Do,"* suggests that couples ought to sit down and more or less conduct job interviews with each other before they marry. That may sound cold and unromantic, but the idea provides a great way to find the answer to every couple's most important question: What do we want our future together to look like?

Outcalt believes that prospective wives and husbands should draw up separate lists of questions, listen carefully for the answers, and prepare themselves for surprises. (If I had actually asked Susan a question about children, I might have learned that her dream about having ten boys was no joke. And that would have been a surprise.)

I think there's merit to Outcalt's proposal, and I urge couples to give it a try. Below I've outlined six broad areas to prompt couples as they prepare questions for each other. A good premarriage conversation should cover each of these areas, and there should be a high comfort level between brides and grooms in all of these areas. If there isn't a high comfort level after the "interview," couples should be prepared to reassess their plans — or at the very least to get some help from a therapist.

Most of us could probably think of these areas — and quite possibly other areas — on our own, but to get the conversation started, let me suggest serious and focused conversation in the following areas:

1. Communication Styles and Patterns

Many couples report that when they first met they stayed up for hours and "just talked." This experience leads them to believe that they have excellent communication skills. But my experience leads me to believe that these early, initial conversations are weak predictors of good communication patterns in a marriage.

Couples should honestly assess — perhaps with the help of a therapist — how they're going to communicate with each other. In their covenant, they should establish ground rules for their conversations about difficult subjects, agreeing together about how, when, and in what way these conversations are going to take place.

In most marriage books I've read, couples in happy relationships have said that they prefer to have scheduled, weekly conversations. In these conversations, each partner has an opportunity to reflect on how things are going, while the other partner is expected to listen without comment. Specific rules about these conversations change over time and need to be assessed frequently, but the point is to get started.

My own church feels so strongly about this issue that it asks couples who will be married in our church to participate in a communication class for couples.

2. Financial Management

Most couples who are married early in their lives bring very little to a marriage beyond student loan debt. But couples who are older or who have been working for a few years have often accumulated substantial assets. In these cases, I ordinarily recommend a prenuptial agreement. Again, this is something that strikes most couples as unromantic, and it appears to assume the worst. But my response is to point to the purchase of life insurance. I don't plan to die; I plan to live. Still, to provide for my family in the event that something happens to me, I believe it's wise to have life insurance. Similarly, a prenuptial agreement can simply be a way to do some responsible planning; it answers many difficult questions at the beginning. When there are grown children from a previous marriage, for example, a prenuptial agreement specifies exactly how the assets are to be divided, especially all those items of sentimental value.

Recently I married a couple who were in their seventies. At first they resisted the idea of a prenuptial agreement, but ultimately they wrote one with the help of a lawyer who is a member of our church. At the wedding, the adult children of both parents thanked me for prodding them to make important financial decisions before the marriage. Knowing how all the assets were going to be divided helped everyone to have a better time at the wedding — and to feel better about the marriage.

An important area for all couples to reach some agreement about is money. Very often partners bring to the marriage two very different ideas about how to spend and how to save money. And studies show that money issues are a frequent source of marital conflict — in some studies the most frequent source.

It's not romantic to talk about money in this kind of detail — I'll grant you that. But couples who don't talk about it before they get married may have very little romance after they get married.

3. Children

I'm amazed by how many couples get married without having discussed whether or not they plan to have children. I shouldn't be, I suppose, given my own experience, but I am.

A generation or two ago, this subject might have been an odd one to raise. Children, after all, were an expected outcome of every marriage, sooner rather than later. Not being able to produce children, in fact, was sometimes a reason to end the marriage. But that's clearly not the case anymore. Today couples often enter marriage with very different expectations regarding children. A couple may decide at the beginning that they don't want to have children. Or a couple may have one partner who wants children and one who doesn't. This is a serious difference of opinion that should be worked out before vows are exchanged.

Once a couple has decided to have children, they should agree on the number of children they think they would like to have (although this number can be subject to revision for a variety of reasons). Related to this discussion is the subject of parenting. Among the questions that ought to be asked are these: Who's going to do the parenting? And how? Will one or both partners take time off from work after a child is born? Recognizing that feelings about children can and do change, what are the expectations at the beginning?

Blended families now seem to be the norm rather than the exception. Couples who don't have conversations (and reach agreements) about their blended families before getting married are courting disaster. Each partner of a couple I married recently brought a few children to the marriage — his were high-school and college age, hers were still in preschool. To their credit, they talked extensively with a therapist about parenting styles and several other related issues. They even brought the children into the conversation. I suspect that their dealing with some of the anticipated problems will make dealing with the unanticipated ones a great deal easier.

4. Sex

In spite of our culture's preoccupation with sex — and what appears to be an unprecedented openness about sex — my experience suggests that couples don't talk all that much about their sex lives and their sexual expectations of each other. Some couples may want to involve a therapist in this conversation; a neutral third party could help them have an open and productive discussion.

5. Family

Family-of-origin issues can be huge factors in a marriage relationship. And in my experience most couples are ill-equipped to explore these issues by themselves. Often — though not always — I see serious family-of-origin issues surface already in the planning of a wedding. This is yet another area where a therapist could provide insights and guidance that would be enormously helpful in the marriage relationship.

Not all issues can be anticipated, of course, but some general principles or priorities can be agreed on. A few summers ago I married a couple who presented an interesting family issue. He grew up in my church, and his family was active both in the church and in the community. In fact, he had uncles and aunts, cousins and other relatives throughout the community. She, on the other hand, grew up in another state, and her family was very small. She rarely saw them. His family looked attractive to her, but it was also intimidating. She wanted to know that their marriage would always come first in his life, and that spending time with his closer, larger family wouldn't preclude spending time with her family. So, early on they reached some agreements about their priorities — how much time they would spend with his family and how often they would travel to be with her family. I doubt that they've avoided all of the possible conflict, but I admired them for recognizing the potential problems at the outset and doing their best to address them.

6. Faith

Of all the issues that are discussed in the weeks and months leading up to a wedding, this is usually the one that gets the least attention. Couples seem to think that it can be dealt with very easily.

In my experience, the opposite is the case. Faith issues can become large obstacles in the years following the wedding, and I wish more couples would take seriously their differences on faith matters from the beginning. Most often, agreeing not to agree results in no religious affiliation at all.

Are there other areas to cover? Undoubtedly. Each couple should identify those other areas where conversations and agreements would be helpful prior to the wedding. The point here is not to be exhaustive but to encourage couples to start talking together, to have discussions that can help them shape a covenant that will be meaningful and helpful to them.

What Keeps a Marriage Going?

Researchers Jeanette and Robert Lauer interviewed three hundred couples who said they were happily married. In addition to being interviewed, they were asked to fill out a questionnaire that included thirty-nine statements about marriage. Couples were asked to select and rank the statements that best described why their marriages had lasted. Men and women filled out the questionnaire separately, but — as the results demonstrate — they showed remarkable agreement on the keys to an enduring relationship. Here are the first fifteen statements ranked in order:

Men	Women
My spouse is my best friend.	My spouse is my best friend.
I like my spouse as a person.	I like my spouse as a person.
Marriage is a long-term commitment.	Marriage is a long-term commitment.
Marriage is sacred.	Marriage is sacred.
We agree on aims and goals.	We agree on aims and goals.
My spouse has grown more interesting.	My spouse has grown more interesting.

<table>
<tr><td>

I want the relationship to succeed.

An enduring marriage is important to social stability.

We laugh together.

I am proud of my spouse's achievements.

We agree on a philosophy of life.

We agree about our sex life.

We agree on how and how often to show affection.

I confide in my spouse.

We share outside hobbies and interests.

</td><td>

I want the relationship to succeed.

We laugh together.

We agree on a philosophy of life.

We agree on how and how often to show affection.

An enduring marriage is important to social stability.

We have a stimulating exchange of ideas.

We discuss things calmly.

We agree about our sex life.

I am proud of my spouse's achievements.

</td></tr>
</table>

A Vow Renewal Ceremony

In celebration of the twenty-fifth wedding anniversary of
Mary R. Talen and Thomas B. Dozeman

The Gathering

Prelude

Procession

Welcome

Opening Prayer

L(eader): We praise you, we worship you, we adore you.

P(eople): You hold the heavens in your hand,
All stars rejoice in your glory.

L: You come in the sunrise and the song of morn
And bless the splendor of noonday.

P: The stars in their courses magnify you.
Day and night tell of your glory.

L: Your peace blows over the earth
And the breath of your mouth fills all space.

P: Your voice comes in the thunder of the storm
And the song of the wind whispers of your majesty.

L: You satisfy all things living with your abundance
And our hearts bow at your presence.

P: Accept us, your children,
And hearken to our prayer.

L: Bend over us, Eternal Love,
and bless us in this celebration of marriage.

A Hymn Response "Joyful, Joyful, We Adore Thee"

The Word

The Gift of Marriage

L: Mary and Thomas have come to renew their
marriage vows
In the presence of God, their family, and friends.
Let us now witness their promises to each other
And surround them with our prayers,
Giving thanks to God for the gift of marriage
And asking God's blessing upon them,
So that they may be strengthened for their continued
life together.

God created us male and female,
And gave us marriage
So that husband and wife may help and comfort
each other,
Living faithfully together in plenty and in want,
In joy and in sorrow,
In sickness and in health,
Throughout all their days.
Love conquers even death itself.

A Reading on the Power of Love Song of Solomon 8:6-7

A Hymn Response "Love Divine, All Loves Excelling"

L: God gave us marriage as a holy mystery.
    In marriage, husband and wife are called to a new
       way of life,
    Created, ordered, and blessed by God.
    In marriage we join with God in love and in the
       dance of life.

A Teaching on the Mystery of Love 1 John 4:7-8

A Hymn Response "The Lord of the Dance"

L: God gave us marriage
    For the full expression of the love between a man
       and a woman.
    In marriage a woman and a man belong to each other,
    And with affection and tenderness
    Freely give themselves to each other.

A Teaching on Marriage from Jesus Mark 10:6-8

A Hymn Response Psalm 126

The Renewal of Marriage Vows

A Prayer

A Song of Blessing

The Giving

An Announcement of Marriage

L: Before God,
    And in your presence
    We have renewed our marriage vows.
    Our love over the last twenty-five years
    Has been enriched and sustained through your gifts to us.
    As a symbol of our mutual love for each other,
    We wish to share a gift with each family present.

[At this point a ceramic tile was presented to each family member.]

A Hymn

The Sending Forth

Chamber Music

A Benediction   Go Now in Peace

APPENDIX D

Mediation: An Alternative to Litigation

What Is Divorce Mediation?

In the past, it has been the generally accepted view that divorcing couples could no longer communicate with each other directly over divorce issues. Instead, they were to keep each other at arm's length, speaking only through their attorneys. Yet the end of a marital relationship does not necessarily end the couple's need to communicate with each other, particularly when they must maintain a relationship as parents of their children.

As the rate of divorce has increased, the demand for a less adversarial and even healing alternative to the old model has developed. Divorce mediation provides a safe, neutral process that allows couples to communicate directly with each other about issues they cannot resolve on their own.

The beauty of mediation is that it allows a couple to communicate cooperatively and fairly about the end of their marital relationship, while avoiding much of the increased hostility, hurt, and pain that are typical by-products of the adversarial legal system. Litigation tends to focus on the couple's past relationship, which generally increases defensiveness and resentment. Mediation, on the other hand, focuses on healthy, cooperative, and controlled communication between the two people at a time when everything seems to be working against that. Mediation allows the divorcing couple to decide how *they* — not the courts — will solve their problems.

The mediator provides support and guidance in designing a plan for their future and the future of their family. Mediation views the couple and their children (if children are involved) as persons whose primary concern in the divorce process is to re-organize their family in such a way as to acknowledge the impor-tance of their original relationship while remaining sensitive to each person's need in the new family structure. If the couple chooses, their children can even be brought into the mediation process to voice their opinion about the parenting decisions that are being made on their behalf.

It is important to understand that mediation does not sub-stitute for attorney representation. A couple who chooses to me-diate their divorce still need to retain individual attorneys to pro-vide legal advice and represent their individual interests in court. The mediator does use the law to guide the couple in their nego-tiations but does not give legal advice. The primary directive of the mediator is to remain neutral throughout the couple's nego-tiations.

How Does Mediation Work?

A couple can begin meeting with a trained mediator either before they have seen an attorney or at any time during the legal divorce process — even after a trial is in progress. There is never a wrong time to mediate if it helps to resolve issues. Together, the couple and the mediator meet and agree, among other things, on the fol-lowing:

- that certain communication ground rules will be followed in order to empower both of the parties equally;
- that the couple's discussions will remain confidential and that the mediator will not be available to testify on behalf of either party if litigation should later occur; and

- that they will each make a good-faith commitment to the process, including the mandatory full disclosure and valuation of all income, assets, and liabilities if the mediation includes the division of assets, spousal maintenance, and/or child-support issues.

Generally, the couple will meet with the mediator for two to eight sessions, depending on the couple's ability to communicate and the complexity of the issues and/or assets involved. Post-judgment mediations tend to take less time because the issues are often fewer and/or more specific. Typically, each session lasts one to two hours, but almost any time arrangement can be made. Mediations can even be conducted by telephone.

The mediator encourages the couple to stay in contact with their attorneys and to seek individual legal and financial advice between sessions so that they can return to mediation with the legal knowledge necessary to make informed decisions. However, the negotiations of the issues and the decisions made regarding their divorce rest with the couple and take into account the needs and interests of all concerned.

When the sessions are completed, the mediator compiles the agreements the parties have made into a "Memorandum of Agreements," which is then given to them. The parties in turn give copies of the memorandum to their attorneys, if a legal case is pending, for legal review and filing with the court.

Susan C. DeYoung, J.D.,
Director of Mediation Services
Central DuPage Pastoral Counseling Center
507A Thornhill Drive
Carol Stream, IL 60188